# LAND MINES
# IN
# EL SALVADOR
# AND
# NICARAGUA

## The Civilian Victims

An Americas Watch Report

December 1986

36 W. 44th St.
New York, NY 10036
212-840-9460

739 Eighth Street, S.E.
Washington, DC 20003
202-546-9336

## AMERICAS WATCH COMMITTEE

The Americas Watch Committee was established by The Fund for
Free Expression in 1981 to monitor and promote observance of
free expression and other internationally recognized human rights
in the Western hemisphere.

Cover Design: Amy Bogert
Cover Photo:  Susan Meiselas
             *Nicaraguan victim of land mine.*

# TABLE OF CONTENTS

i

## ACKNOWLEDGMENTS

The Appendix to this report discussing the laws of war applicable to the use of land mines in El Salvador and Nicaragua was written by Robert Goldman, Professor of Law and Louis James Scholar at American University. The rest of this report was written by Jemera Rone, Anne Nelson and Aryeh Neier and is based on research conducted in El Salvador and Nicaragua by Jemera Rone.

Americas Watch is grateful to the many persons who provided us with information for this report. In varying degree, they include representatives of the Salvadoran government, the Nicaraguan government, the Salvadoran rebels and the Nicaraguan rebels.

We are particularly grateful to the many victims of land mines -- those who had been injured themselves and those who lost members of their families -- who provided us with information.

# INTRODUCTION

Since the beginning of 1982, the Americas Watch has published more than a score of reports on human rights in El Salvador and Nicaragua. Throughout that period military conflicts have been underway in both countries. All of our reports on these two countries have dealt with abuses of human rights that are related to those conflicts, but our primary concern has been the victimization of civilians taking no active part in hostilities.

In the past two years, the use of land mines has emerged as a significant cause of civilian casualties in both countries. Previous Americas Watch reports on both countries have discussed this problem, but we determined to deal with it more extensively both because of the increasing incidence with which civilians are being killed and maimed and because of the complexity of the issues raised by mining in international law.

This report sets forth our analysis of the applicable international law and our findings on the practices of the parties to the conflicts in El Salvador and Nicaragua. Americas Watch finds that:

1

1. International law prohibits the use of mines in a manner in which they have been used extensively in both El Salvador and Nicaragua. That is, in both countries, mines have been placed in areas known to be used by civilians without effective markings or other effective warnings. Some mines have not been removed and none of the mines self-destruct once their military purpose has been served. Such uses violate international law;

2. In El Salvador, mines have been used by both sides to the conflict in areas frequented by civilians. The circumstances of their placement, the testimony Americas Watch has gathered, the findings of the Roman Catholic Archdiocese and its human rights office, Tutela Legal, and the findings of independent journalists, all persuade us that, in the main, civilian casualties result from mines placed by the FMLN guerrillas. In some cases, this is because the guerrillas do not provide adequate warnings, or do not remove mines after they serve their military objectives. In other cases, warnings may cover a wide area, but are not specific enough to be effective. In still other cases, warnings are given but desperately poor peasants take risks, and suffer the consequences, because they urgently require food or firewood.

We have not found that either side to the conflict in El Salvador deliberately uses mines against civilians. It is the indiscriminate use of mines to which we object;

3. In Nicaragua, the circumstances of the placement of mines, the testimony we have gathered, and the findings of independent journalists all persuade us that it is mining by the rebels (*contras*) that has caused the great majority of civilian casualties. We are aware of civilian casualties in just one incident within Nicaragua that are attributable to Nicaraguan government mining. On the other hand, additional civilian casualties have occurred across the border in Honduras as a result of Nicaraguan government mining.

The *contras* do not provide warnings about their use of mines. We do not know whether they have removed any mines after they served their military objectives. The circumstances in Nicaragua indicate that mines probably have been used deliberately against civilians by the *contras*. Their placement, the use of antitank contact mines on highways traversed by civilian vehicles, the failure to provide any warnings and an episode in which the *contras* fired on injured survivors of a mine explosion suggest that killing civilians is probably one of the purposes of their mining. At the least, the *contras* have used mines indiscriminately.

We have information on sporadic Nicaraguan government mining in Honduras. The circumstances that we know about suggest that such mining is not used deliberately against civilians but the lack of warnings indicates that mines are used indiscriminately;

3

4. In sum, government and rebel forces in both El Salvador and Nicaragua have used land mines indiscriminately; government forces of both countries have used land mines sporadically and rebel forces have used them extensively in both countries; and the evidence suggests that the *contras* in Nicaragua probably have used mines deliberately against civilians.

Americas Watch condemns the deliberate use of mines against civilians which, we find, has probably been practiced by the rebels (*contras*) in Nicaragua; we condemn the rebels (FMLN) in El Salvador and the *contras* in Nicaragua for their extensive indiscriminate use of mines that kill and maim civilians; we condemn the Salvadoran Armed Forces for the sporadic episodes in which we believe that Salvadoran civilians have been killed and maimed as a consequence of their indiscriminate use of mines; and we condemn the Nicaraguan Armed Forces for the sporadic episodes in which civilians in Honduras have been killed and maimed by their indiscriminate use of mines.

It should be noted that the U.S. government has vigorously condemned the mining practices of the Salvadoran guerrillas but has either remained silent about the practices of the Nicaraguan rebels or has attempted to cast doubt on reports of civilian casualties attributable to those practices. Because the evidence indicates the the *contras* probably make deliberate efforts to kill civilians by the use of land mines, their practices warrant particularly severe condemnation.

Americas Watch calls on all parties to the wars in Central America to limit their use of land mines so as to avoid civilian casualties.

## STANDARDS

As the Americas Watch has noted in previous reports, the standards against which we assess the conduct of governments and the rebel forces combatting them are the laws of war applicable to the conflicts in El Salvador and Nicaragua. These are derived principally from Article 3 common to the 1949 Geneva Conventions, which were ratified by both countries; and from Protocol II additional to the Geneva Conventions, which has been ratified by El Salvador. These are provisions of the laws of war that apply expressly to internal armed conflicts.

In assessing the use of land mines in the conflicts in El Salvador and Nicaragua, Americas Watch is again guided by these provisions of international law. In addition we are guided by a Protocol on the use of land mines and booby traps that was annexed to the 1981 United Nations Convention on the use of weapons that are considered "excessively injurious" and that have "indiscriminate effects." Though that U.N. convention applies expressly to international wars, as we discuss in the Appendix to this report, we consider that it is also an appropriate source of rules that should be used to measure the conduct of the warring parties in El Salvador and Nicaragua. In this section, we refer to that Protocol as the Land Mines Protocol or simply as the Protocol. (See the Appendix for full titles and legal citations.)

The United Nations Land Mines Protocol does not prohibit the use of land mines and similar weapons against military targets, but it does try to protect civilians from their effects.

The two main sources of civilian mining casualties are mines that are planted in regions populated by civilians, and mines that remain active after they have outlasted their military utility, presenting an ongoing threat to civilians.

The Land Mines Protocol tries to protect civilians in three ways. These are:

1. by helping to define the difference between civilian and military targets;

2. by prohibiting indiscriminate use of land mines and by governing the way they are used against military targets;

3. by requiring precautionary measures to avoid or minimize civilian casualties that result from attacks against military targets.

**Prohibitions**

The Land Mines Protocol prohibits all direct use of land mines, booby traps, or related devices against a civilian population or individual civilians.

1. A "mine" is defined as any munition placed under, on, or

near the ground that is designed to be set off by the contact or approach of a person or a vehicle. A "remotely delivered mine" can be fired from a weapon or dropped from an aircraft.

2. A "booby-trap" is any weapon that is meant to go off when a person touches or approaches an apparently harmless object.

3. "Other devices" means any munition that is set off by remote control or goes off automatically after a lapse of time.

A civilian is defined as anyone who does not actively participate in attacks intended to cause physical harm to enemy personnel or objects. The Protocol adds that the presence of a small number of off-duty combatants in a civilian community does not make that community eligible for attacks, including the use of land mines. "Civilian objects" are anything that does not belong to the military or make a direct contribution for a military purpose.

The Protocol prohibits the "indiscriminate" or "blind" use of land mines and similar weapons. This means any situation where the combatant who plants the mine has no way of reasonably guessing whether it will be triggered by an enemy combatant or a civilian. Officially, "indiscriminate" is defined as a weapon that is not aimed at a military objective; a weapon that is not capable of being aimed at a specific military objective; or a weapon that can be expected to cause incidental civilian casualties and damage that is excessive in relation to the anticipated military advantage to be gained. The Protocol adds that "blind weapons" can also include land mines that are laid without precautions, unrecorded, unmarked, and left behind after they have outlasted their military usefulness, since civilians could trigger them years after the war has ended.

The Protocol calls upon combatants to warn civilians of the placement of land mines wherever possible. It prohibits the use of hand-delivered mines and booby-traps in any area containing a civilian population where combat is not taking place, unless:

a. the mines are placed on or near a military objective under the control of the enemy; or

b. measures are taken to protect the civilians, such as by posting warning signs, posting sentries, issuing warnings, or putting up fences.

This prohibition does not extend to any village or area where combat between ground forces is taking place or is about to take place.

There are special provisions for "remotely delivered mines," which include any mine that is launched from a weapon or dropped from an aircraft. These mines can only be used in an area that is in itself a military objective, or which contains a military objective. Even then, they cannot be used unless their location can be accurately recorded, or unless each mine can be turned off or can self-destruct by remote control after it outlasts its military purpose.

For pre-planned minefields and booby-traps, combatants are required to follow certain guidelines: First, they must make maps and diagrams to show the extent of the mined area. Second, they must decide on a single reference point and define the mined area in relation to that reference point. These diagrams should be as specific as possible.

Booby-traps are devices that are designed to look like innocent objects that explode when they are touched or approached.

There are strict rules governing the use of booby-traps. They cannot be made in the form of an apparently harmless portable object, which rules out the use of mass-produced prefabricated booby-traps, as well as booby-traps dropped *en masse* from aircraft.

The Protocol also forbids any use of booby traps in any way associated with:

1. internationally recognized protective emblems, signs or signals (such as a chemical, electrical, or nuclear danger sign identifying a facility that could release "dangerous forces" that could result in severe casualties to civilians);

2. sick, wounded or dead persons;

3. burial sites or graves;

4. medical facilities, medical equipment, medical supplies or medical transportation;

5. children's toys or anything else specially designed for the feeding, health, hygiene, clothing or education of children;

6. food or drink;

7. kitchen utensils or appliances (except in military establishments or military locations);

8. objects clearly of a religious nature;

9. historic monuments, works of art or places or worship that are part of a people's cultural or spiritual heritage;

10. animals or their carcasses.

These prohibitions share the common goal of attempting to respect civilians, cultural property, and the sick and wounded. For the ways the Land Mines Protocol and related conventions relate specifically to El Salvador and Nicaragua, see the Appendix to this report.

## EL SALVADOR

As the war in El Salvador drags into its eighth year, both government forces and guerrillas have sought new weapons and new methods to adapt to tactical shifts in the confrontation. Recently, land mines have become a significant factor in the war; their use has increased sharply over the last two years, and there has been a corresponding increase in the number of civilians killed and wounded by the mines.

Many of the casualties take place in remote rural areas, and casualty figures can vary. Over 1985, Tutela Legal documented 31 civilian dead by mining, while the U.S. Embassy listed 43. The two sources are in closer agreement for early 1986; Tutela Legal counted 38 civilian deaths for the first six months of the year, while the Embassy lists 36. (For prior Americas Watch reports of mining, see "The Continuing Terror," pp. 79-80 and 121-23, September 1985; and "Settling into Routine," pp. 72-75, May 1986.) Many more civilians are wounded than killed by the mining, but definite figures for the injured are even more difficult to ascertain.

There is no evidence to suggest that either the Salvadoran

government or the guerrilla forces are intentionally targeting the civilian population in their placement of land mines. The increase in civilian casualties is far more likely the result of careless and negligent military practices, particularly the failure to warn adequately the civilian population that a given area is mined. The FMLN bears greater responsibility than the Armed Forces because it uses mines more extensively and, apparently, more indiscriminately, but both sides share in the blame.

Mines are sometimes set off in areas where both government and guerrilla forces are present, making it difficult to pin responsibility with certainty on one party. In a few cases, recorded deaths and injuries cannot be considered to violate the rules of war in the sense that they involve civilians who entered mined areas despite warnings, with what we can only term reckless disregard of warning signs. Most of the survivors in this category said that although they knew the area was conflictive, they were poor and needed to travel through it in search of food or firewood. In some cases, which are more problematic so far as the rules of war are concerned, they also state that the warnings concerned a general area, not a specific place.

The use of land mines cannot be analyzed outside the overall context of military strategy. Mines are a prototypical weapon for guerrilla forces, serving to defend rural-based insurgents with the same specificity as government forces' aerial bombardments are designed to dislodge them. Land mines are a logical response to classic counterinsurgency doctrine, which prescribes incessant army foot patrols to wear the guerrillas down. The guerrillas anticipate the path of the advancing patrols and sow mines designed to injure on contact, disrupting the patrols and demoralizing the troops, who then hesitate to patrol aggressively.

Salvadoran guerrillas have also used mines in ambushes and, more rarely, in booby traps; they often employ them to block entry to FMLN-controlled zones and supply lines. These mines accomplish their objectives: Salvadoran Armed Forces casualties from mining have risen sharply in 1986, far outnumbering civilian casualties. The Armed Forces of El Salvador also use mines, although mines are less to the government's advantage and their use is correspondingly more limited. Government forces tend to use mines defensively to protect their emplacements, but they also use mines (including contact mines) offensively in ambushes and in locations where the FMLN is likely to set up camp or pass by.

Each side has held the other responsible for the civilian casualties that have resulted from the escalating use of mines. But unlike aerial bombardment, a tactic that is available only to the Armed Forces, mines are used by both sides. Government and guerrilla forces sometimes employ mines of similar design -- the Armed Forces will improvise mines when manufactured mines are not available.

The Archbishop of San Salvador, Monsignor Arturo Rivera y Damas, has condemned the use of mines and holds the FMLN primarily responsible, as does the Americas Watch. In his February 9, 1986 homily the Archbishop named three civilian victims of FMLN mining (although there is some factual dispute as to whether all three were actually victims of FMLN mining). He called upon "the members of the FMLN not to locate mines in places frequented by the civilian population, because in the majority of the cases, innocent victims result from the explosion of these devices." He added, in the next breath, "We make the same insistent call for an end to the indiscriminate bombings in

13

zones inhabited by the civilian population."

Land mines have become a serious problem for the civilian population in El Salvador. If both sides do not take firm steps to change their mining practices, they will bequeath their country generations of victims, in the form of civilians who will stumble over mines whose location has long since been forgotten by those who planted them for their military enemies.

## Background

The increase in land mines and their civilian casualties is directly related to questions of El Salvador's displaced population and its land tenure crisis.

El Salvador is a tiny, densely populated country with a largely agrarian economy, and as a result the competition to own and utilize land is intense. Land hunger has been a central issue in the still-unresolved social conflict that led to the war, and the war has aggravated this land hunger by devastating large stretches of land and displacing the poorest of the poor from many rural areas.[1]

In the early 1980s the FMLN gained a political and military momentum that the Armed Forces could not effectively combat until they received substantial U.S. funds and training. Since the onset of the war, three types of territory have developed: government-controlled areas, FMLN-controlled areas (which the government calls "areas of persistence"), and disputed or conflicted zones.

The FMLN has mined some key areas under its control in order to protect its rear guard, especially since it lacks sanctuary in bordering countries. The guerrillas declare the mined areas

14

off limits to the civilian population, which has the effect of displacing more people; this is evident from the interviews we cite below.

The war has created a large, fluid population of displaced persons in El Salvador, and has made significant areas of the scarce fertile land impossible to farm. The populated areas of FMLN zones have received displaced people who are FMLN supporters or who feared government persecution. They resettled alongside peasants who were native to the region and who either supported the FMLN or coexisted with whichever armed force was dominant at a given time. Most government supporters left or were pushed out by the FMLN.

The Armed Forces have displaced large numbers of people from the FMLN controlled zones and conflicted zones. These operations have resulted in many civilian victims and the destruction of food and property. The last recorded large-scale massacre took place in August 1984 at the Gualsinga River in Chalatenango, an FMLN-controlled territory, where some 50 civilians were killed by advancing government troops. Such incursions on the part of the Armed Forces prompted the guerrillas to make increasing use of mines to protect the territory they controlled.

A number of peasants fled the conflict regions of El Salvador between 1983 and 1985 in response to a series of aerial bombardments that took a grave toll in civilians killed and wounded and property damage. As late as 1986, roving helicopters aimed machine-gun fire at peasants trying to till the fields, and the Armed Forces frequently burned their crops. Some civilians stayed on, however, because of fear or poverty: in the FMLN-controlled zones and in many conflicted zones, the peasants farm rent-free land in a kind of *de facto* land reform.

The latest wave of displacement has taken place over 1985 and 1986, with the military's forced relocation of large numbers of civilians. This process, which is an attempt to deny the FMLN a civilian population base, is known as "draining the sea," and is usually implemented in tandem with permanent roving army patrols in the area.

There have also been efforts to reverse the flow of population for strategic benefit. The Salvadoran government's counter-insurgency program has always included plans to move its civilian supporters, organized in civil defense groups, onto newly-reconquered land in order to secure it. This project was integrated into the so-called National Plan of 1983, which foundered from the Armed Forces' inability to secure the areas in question for any length of time. The Armed Forces now have their own program, called "United to Reconstruct" (*Unidos para Reconstruir*), which bears many similarities to the National Plan.

As of early 1986, both the government and the guerrillas have begun to encourage their allies and neutral parties to repopulate some of the abandoned zones and begin farming them again, as a step towards economic revitalization and increased military control of the disputed areas. In addition, many people go into conflicted areas on their own in search of food or firewood. Both groups become potential mine victims. Land mines have become a factor in preventing repopulation of territory that the FMLN controls.

Americas Watch considers that civilians should not be used as a wedge for one side to gain entry in the territory of the other. Because of the dangers to civilians, we urge that repopulation efforts should take place when both sides have been persuaded to agree to the undertaking.

This is not impossible; in Tenancingo, the Archbishop has negotiated with both sides to agree to permit the repopulation project to proceed and to abstain from placing any military facilities in the town. Although the town remains technically in dispute, it enjoys a *de facto* cease-fire that allows development by a private nonprofit agency. The Tenancingo project could serve as a useful model for future repopulation efforts. The government should bear in mind that the role of nongovernment agencies is essential in order to avoid speculation that the government promotes repopulation solely for its military advantage. Also, repopulation projects sponsored by nongovernmental groups are more likely to be free of the mechanisms for surveillance and regimentation that have characterized repopulation under military auspices in neighboring Guatemala. (See Americas Watch's reports on Guatemala, especially "No Neutrals Allowed," November 1982; "A Nation of Prisoners," January 1984; and "Civil Patrols in Guatemala," August 1986.)

War, displacement, overpopulation, counterinsurgency tactics, economic pressures, and land mines combine to make life grimmer than usual for the rural poor of El Salvador. Dealing with land mines alone will by no means remove or resolve the basic issues in dispute, but curbing abusive mining practices will help to alleviate the situation for the Salvadorans who must live within it.

## The Numbers

Although any discussion of human rights issues in El Salvador generates some disagreement as to figures and sources, civilian land mine casualty figures do not vary as greatly as some other categories. The four primary sources for these figures are the Catholic Church agency Tutela Legal, the Salvadoran government's Human Rights Commission, the U.S. Embassy (which cites press clippings, themselves almost always based on Army press releases) and the Armed Forces. In the first six months of 1986, the listings for mine-related civilians deaths ranged from 20 to 47, as follows:

|                | Jan | Feb | Mar | Apr | May | June |
|----------------|-----|-----|-----|-----|-----|------|
| U.S. Embassy   | 2   | 8   | 1   | 15  | 8   | 2    |
| Tutela Legal   | 4   | 8   | 1   | 15  | 8   | 2    |
| Government HRC | 7   | 10  | 2   | 13  | 12  | 3    |
| Armed Forces   | 3   | 3   | 1   | 6   | 6   | 2    |

The total civilian dead from mining for the first six months of 1986 is:

| | |
|----------------|----|
| U.S. Embassy   | 36 |
| Tutela Legal   | 38 |
| Government HRC | 47 |
| Armed Forces   | 21 |

Interestingly enough, the greatest disparity in these figures lies between those reported by the government Human Rights

18

Commission and those from the Armed Forces, the Commission listing 47 deaths to the Armed Forces' 21. There is no significant dispute about the numbers of dead between the U.S. Embassy and Tutela Legal. (The U.S. Embassy counted 3 civilian mining deaths in July; Tutela Legal tabulated 5 civilian mining deaths in July; 3 in August; and 3 in September; the Government Human Rights Commission tabulated 6 in July and 4 in August; and the Armed Forces tabulated none in July. The effects of the earthquake may be responsible for delays in assembling more up-to-date figures.)

The real dispute concerns responsibility. The U.S. Embassy attributed all but one of the deaths listed from January to March 1986 to the FMLN. The government Human Rights Commission blamed the FMLN for all the deaths, including one which both the U.S. Embassy and Tutela Legal agreed was the responsibility of the Armed Forces. The Armed Forces held the FMLN responsible for seven deaths over that period. Tutela Legal attributed one of the victims it reported to the FMLN; the others were listed as unknown.

The U.S. Embassy attributed all 15 dead in April 1986 to FMLN mines. For that same month, Tutela Legal attributed two dead to Armed Forces mines and 13 to undetermined elements. Among the undetermined deaths listed by Tutela were three children from Tecoluca, who picked up a grenade thinking it was a plaything, and were killed when it went off. The Armed Forces had passed through the area that morning, and the most likely explanation for the incident was that one of the soldiers accidentally dropped the grenade.

It is difficult to pin down the responsibility in such cases. To our knowledge, only Tutela Legal has attempted to investigate

19

each case by talking to relatives, local authorities, and witnesses. The government Human Rights Commission cites press reports as well as statements by relatives and information from local justices of the peace (who are also cited by Tutela Legal). The U.S. Embassy admits that its information on mining casualties is drawn exclusively from newspaper reports based on Armed Forces press releases.[2]

Whatever the debate over specific figures, Americas Watch believes that the majority of civilian casualties, both wounded and dead, are the result of FMLN-placed mines, primarily due to the FMLN's more frequent use of mines and its inadequate warning system.

**Civilian injuries**

The number of civilians injured by mines is reprehensibly high, regardless of whose figures are credible and who is responsible for these injuries.

The available figures on injuries are all from government or pro-government sources:[4]

It should also be noted that, until they started collecting statistics on civilians wounded by FMLN mining, neither the U.S. Embassy, the Armed Forces, nor the government Human Rights Commission collected any statistical information on civilians injured from any other causes, such as bombing or torture. The interest these groups show in civilian injuries is quite recent, and is focussed on civilian mining victims attributed to the FMLN.

20

|  | Jan | Feb | Mar | Apr | May | June | Totals |
|---|---|---|---|---|---|---|---|
| U.S. Embassy | 12 | 37 | 22 | 28 | 28 | 14 | 141 |
| Govt HRC | 17 | 32 | 26 | 29 | 20 | 26 | 150 |
| Armed Forces | 17 | 19 | 26 | 24 | 10 | 14 | 110 |

The U.S. Embassy tabulated an additional 12 civilian mining injuries in July; the government Human Rights Commission counted 22 in July and 8 in August; and the Armed Forces counted 6 in July. (Again, the effects of the earthquake appear to have delayed the compilation of more up-to-date data.)

The number of wounded is several times the number of dead from mining: according to the U.S. Embassy and the government Human Rights Commission,[5] about three times as many; according to the Armed Forces, five times as many.

The figures that are available suggest that the number of civilians killed and wounded by land mines reached its highest point in April 1986. The decline in deaths and injuries thereafter was confirmed by our own spot checks in regional hospitals. We do not know whether the decline reflects a decreasing use of land mines, increased care by civilians to avoid areas that may be mined, the advent of the rainy season (May to November) or some combination of these.

**Military Casualties**

Obviously, both government and guerrilla forces place mines to inflict military casualties. Precise figures are not available for Armed Forces mining casualties. The head of the Military Hospital in San Salvador told us, however, that the Armed

Forces' medical evacuation procedures have improved substantially and that there are now very few military deaths from mining incidents. The military's personnel wounded by mines far outnumber those killed by mines.

Many more soldiers than civilians are wounded by mines in El Salvador, although it is difficult to get a precise figure. Americas Watch has received reports varying from 517 to over 1000 Armed Forces personnel injured by mines over the first eight months of 1986. This is far larger than the civilian injured count for the first six months of 1986, which government sources placed at figures ranging from 110 to 150.

Based on these uncertain figures, the military injury rate from mines runs from about 64 to 125 a month, while the civilian rate is between 19 and 25 a month. One high-ranking official at the Military Hospital in San Salvador told us that they received at least one military mine-injury case a day, and often more. A tour of the military hospital wards confirmed the tragic prevalence of permanent injuries from mines. There was a large number of amputees, far more than in the civilian hospitals we visited.[6]

Officials from the Joint Chiefs of Staff have stated that last year 40 to 45 percent of their wounded resulted from mining. In 1986, the rate rose to 65 percent. The most conservative estimate of this year's proportion of mining injuries to total military injuries we heard was 60 percent; the Military Hospital in San Salvador estimated it was closer to 80 percent.

There are additional, sometimes conflicting, figures on the number of soldiers wounded by mines. Since both sets of figures are from good sources, we will quote them as background and as an additional illustration of the difficulty in obtaining consistent

22

statistics in El Salvador even from allied parties.

The Military Hospital in San Salvador, which has 400 beds (compared to the only other similar military medical facility, in San Miguel, with 100 beds) reports that 1006 soldiers were treated for mining injuries from January 1 to August 20, 1986 in that hospital alone.[7]

Another reliable source has informed us that 517 soldiers were wounded by mines in the first eight months of 1986; of these, 280 need artificial legs. The U.S. government has undertaken an impressive program to provide wounded military personnel with prosthetic limbs and rehabilitation, and to train Salvadorans in special skills to aid them. Unfortunately, there is no similar program available for civilian mine victims.

### FMLN Mining Practices and Violations

The purpose of FMLN land mines is to injure and kill government soldiers, in order to prevent them from retaking territory held by the FMLN, and to impede their search-and-destroy missions. Army authorities have voiced the opinion that the guerrillas intentionally use mines to maim soldiers, producing a high incidence of amputees, to demoralize the troops.

We believe that the FMLN's extensive use of mines is a response to the Armed Forces' escalation of foot patrols in conflict zones, in accordance with the classic counterinsurgency strategy of keeping the guerrillas on the run.

Although the guerrillas claim that they try to warn civilians of the mines, such warnings as exist are not adequate. In addition, civilians apparently disregard general warnings and warning signs and venture into conflicted areas.

23

There is no indication that the FMLN has targeted civilians with its mines. At least one knowledgeable officer in the Armed Forces agrees with this assessment, and expressed his hope that, when the FMLN recognized the extent of the injury to civilians caused by FMLN mining, it would alter its practices. One relief official told us that he believed that the high commands of both the Armed Forces and the FMLN wished to avoid civilian injury by mines, but that injuries continued to take place because of careless practices by lower-ranking personnel. This observer had no doubt that the FMLN warns people away from areas that are mined, but peasants go into these areas nonetheless to farm and gather wood. In his experience, the FMLN takes public responsibility for the mines it has placed, but in some cases the guerrillas deny government charges.

An FMLN broadcast on Radio Venceremos on July 31, 1986 outlined the ways in which the FMLN uses mines. It stated that the FMLN locates mines in the path of the enemy; when the enemy has withdrawn, the terrain is screened to deactivate unexploded mines. The FMLN broadcast claimed that the guerrillas never leave the mines behind, and criticized the Army for doing so. Our research indicates the FMLN does leave mines behind, however.

Guerrillas told one relief worker that their method of recording mine locations was to charge the individual who placed the mine to remember where it is and remove it after the operation. Among the flaws in this method are that the individual may be killed, or the Army may control access to the zone, making mine removal impossible.

Another glimpse of guerrilla policy on mines may be provided by a document entitled "*Armamento Popular*." The

24

document, purportedly captured from the FMLN on May 10, 1986 in San Agustín, Usulután, is now being distributed by the U.S. Embassy. It has the look of authenticity because it describes practices that have been independently observed; even so, it must be viewed cautiously until the FMLN acknowledges authorship. The document makes it clear that the guerrillas employ explosives as a measure against the Armed Forces, not civilians. It states that there is to be no mining in areas frequented by the civilian population, except in the case of an Army offensive, and then with advance warning. It instructs that mines are to be removed, and prescribes detailed safety precautions. These measures are in keeping with the guidelines we would propose for the use of mines. However, the captured document also suggests the placement of mines as booby traps, in violation of such guidelines.

It classifies "weapons of the people" into three categories: contact bombs, Molotov cocktails, and mines. Contact bombs and Molotov cocktails are intended to be thrown at enemy troops and other military objectives.

Mines are designed to deter the advance of the government troops. The document states: "Mines: these are what we use to wear down enemy forces in action, when they are dispatched on foot to their daily positions."

The captured document lists various types of mines: *mina de chuchito* (clothespin mine); *mina abanico* (fan mine); and *mina de pateo* (or *quita pata*, literally, kicked mine or mine that removes feet); alternately known by the guerrilla name, *mina Atlacatl.* This list does not cover the entire range of mines the FMLN has fabricated. Even Army officers give the FMLN some credit for the ingenuity of the wide variety of mines it has sown in their soldiers' path.  Additional types of mines appear to be variations on the three kinds described in the document.

The document states that the *mina de chuchito* is triggered by a wire stretched across a path.  It should be located on paths or ravines and, when the enemy is not using the paths, in the underbrush.  It can also be placed on different objects, such as a body, a sausage, on the door of a house, in a vehicle, or among propaganda leaflets.

The *mina de pateo* is triggered by contact or pressure, such as a footstep.  The document states that the mines should be placed in the path of the enemy on trails, at the entrance to a house, and on the way to wells.  It should be placed in areas where the civilian population does not go: in command posts, in enemy positions such as trenches, on heights the enemy is likely to occupy upon arrival in an area, and in places where they might deposit support arms.

Security measures for the *mina de pateo* say specifically that "in places where a civilian population is present, never mine, unless there is a confirmed enemy advance."

This mine is intended to be removed once the troops have moved on.  The security instructions say clearly that the guerrillas must not forget where they have placed the mine.

The *mina abanico* is intended for use in ambushing convoys.  It is detonated by hand.

On November 10, 1986, in an article by Stephen Kinzer, *The New York Times* reported an interview with Shafik Handal, an FMLN leader, about the use of land mines by his forces.  Mr. Handal is quoted as saying that, "A propaganda campaign has been launched because of the use of mines, trying to make it a human rights issue .... This campaign is aimed at forcing us to renounce a weapon that has been very important to us." Handal is also quoted as acknowledging that, "The mines occasionally produce accidents with the population and also with our own fighters .... We are making an effort to control this."

## Case Studies of FMLN Mining

### Jucuarán, Usulután

There have been a number of civilian injuries and deaths due to mining in the area of Jucuarán over 1986, and the village's profile provides a good background for understanding the many forces that figure in the mining issue. Until early 1986, this remote settlement of some 3000 inhabitants was an FMLN-controlled town. Military authorities have long considered its location in south central Usulután and its mountainous coastline a key drop-off point for FMLN supplies arriving by sea. Local residents say that the dominant guerrilla groups in this region are the Revolutionary Army of the People (ERP) and, to a lesser extent, the Communist Party's Armed Force of Liberation (FAL). The FMLN appears to have lost some civilian support in the area due to its practices of blowing up bridges and downing telephone poles, which has deprived the town of electricity and running water for the past four years.

The Army has stepped up its presence over the year, passing through in patrols and, most recently, it set up a post in town. The Army is blamed for capturing and killing innocent civilians in the early years of the conflict. In 1984 the Air Force bombed the nearby canton of El Zapote, taking it back from the guerrillas, but in the process killing a number of civilians and causing the rest to flee.

For the past two years, the guerrillas have mined a number of areas around Jucuarán. They have forbidden civilians to go into these areas, some of which were deserted after government attacks.

A government civilian employee who has been working in the zone for several years and a local religious leader both told us that the people who live there generally know which areas are considered off limits and possibly mined. He said that the guerrillas prohibit people from entering those areas, but that sometimes people ignore the warnings because they want to work the fields.

One recent mining victim from Jucuarán was José Maria Alemán Moreno, 38, a farmer who was renting land about a kilometer south of town. On August 11, 1986, at about 9 a.m., Alemán stepped on a mine that was planted in a rockpile on the rented farmland. He lost his right leg from the knee down, and received injuries in the left leg and the right hand from shrapnel. The spot was about a hundred yards from a military outpost, and, according to Alemán, a soldier was slightly wounded by a fragment of the same mine.

Alemán said that he had heard no warning that there were mines so close to town, and did not know who planted the mine. The area was adjacent to districts the guerrillas had placed off limits in 1983. Although it is possible that the soldiers could have mined defensively around the perimeter of their post the night before and forgot to remove the mine the next day, it does not seem likely. Most of the local residents we interviewed believed that it was a guerrilla mine, citing other recent injuries in mining incidents.

Another mining victim from the region was José Héctor González Arrieta, 40, who was blinded by what he believed to have been an FMLN mine on July 25, 1986. González was originally from the canton of El Zapote, which was placed off limits by the FMLN several years ago, obliging him to move to a neighboring canton called El Gualora.

González was working as a day laborer picking beans when, at 5 p.m., he touched off the mine while bending down to crawl under a wire fence. Besides being blinded, González was struck by shrapnel on the face and left arm. He told us that he did not know there were mines in the field; however, another man had been killed by a mine nearby, and other mines had been discovered when cattle set them off.

According to González, there is no military post in the area, but the troops pass through, which is why the FMLN plants the mines. The guerrillas told various people that the mines were there, but he emphasized that they had not specified that they were in the spot where he was working.

Circumstances indicate that this mine was left by the FMLN, based on their long-term presence in the area and their prohibition of entry to the adjacent cantons. It appears that the FMLN did warn local residents about the mines. But we were unable to visit the spot and find out whether residents were sufficiently warned, because the local military commander in Jucuarán forbade us to visit the field where the mining took place, or indeed any areas south of Jucuarán, including areas residents told us were safe. (Americas Watch was also prevented by the Armed Forces from investigating some other incidents of alleged guerrilla mining at the sites, but we have subsequently discussed this matter with General Blandón and have been assured of better access in the future.)

## San Marcos Lempa, Usulután

According to an Army explosives expert familiar with the area, the zone north of San Marcos Lempa, including the canton known as 14 de Julio, is very conflictive and heavily mined by the guerrillas. No civilians live in the immediate area. The strategic focal point is the bridge over the Lempa River, which is guarded by both a military post and civil defense.

We talked to two victims of land mines in the San Marcos area; both believed the mines were left by the FMLN.

María Encarnación López Vásquez, 14, the youngest in a family of ten children, set out on May 23, 1986, with four friends to pick mangos. They were walking down a trail used by oxcarts when she stepped on a mine. Her left leg was blown off in the explosion. Her companions, who were walking in front of her, were not injured by the blast.

López said that the guerrillas come to the area to try to blow up the bridge and to shoot at the soldiers. Both the Armed Forces and the guerrillas come through the area, but the guerrillas are there more frequently.

There had been three previous mining incidents very near the spot where the mine was laid. (A woman was injured, a boy lost both arms, and a man was killed, the death taking place just fifteen days before López was hurt.) After these incidents, the guerrillas acknowledged that there were mines in the area, and said they removed them on May 18. Thus López and her companions thought it was safe to go into the area to pick mangos. Her injury was apparently the result of an inadequate removal operation.

On July 27, 1986, José Aguedo Rosa, 40, went hunting in a rural area some ten kilometers north of San Marcos Lempa on a homestead called Hacienda San Juan Letrando. He knew the area, if not the hacienda itself, had been the site of frequent skirmishes, bombings, and land mine incidents (though not on the Hacienda itself). But Aguedo's family was poor, and he was compelled to hunt rabbits and lizards to feed his pregnant wife and four children.

About 9 a.m., he stepped on a mine that was concealed in a heap of leaves and garbage. The explosion broke his left calf, injured his left thigh, and left shrapnel fragments in various parts of his body. He lay helpless all day, fearing death, until, by chance, some patrolling soldiers from the Atonal Battalion discovered him and took him to the hospital. The soldiers detonated three other mines in the same pile of garbage. Aguedo believes that the mines were left by the FMLN some time before. He said that he had heard no warning that the area was mined.

### Apástepeque, San Vicente

Apástepeque, San Vicente is another area that has sustained civilian casualties from land mines. We interviewed one recent victim, Luis Felipe Rodríguez Panameña, 23, in Rosales Hospital in San Salvador.

Rodríguez Panameña lost the lower half of his right leg to a mine blast on May 25, 1986. The explosion occurred in the canton of El Carrizo, near Apástepeque, San Vicente, about two meters from the Pan American Highway. There is a military post a block away, and the area experiences frequent skirmishes.

31

Rodríguez believes that the guerrillas left the mine. He had heard no warning that the area was mined, although civilians were killed and wounded by guerrilla mines the previous year nearby. Shortly after Rodríguez was hurt, a woman passing near the same place stepped on a mine that blew off her legs. Friends visiting Rodríguez at the hospital told him that she died a few days later.

Shortly after interviewing Rodríguez, Americas Watch representatives were able to visit the spot where he was wounded. By chance we met a relative of the victim, who led us to the site of the mine. The relative confirmed that the guerrillas had given no warnings of the mines, and that a woman had been killed nearby. He added that the guerrillas had left mines in the fields alongside the highway; local residents noticed one and asked the government soldiers to remove it, which they did. The relative stated that the soldiers do not leave mines in that area.

### Guadalupe and Chirilagua, San Miguel

An Americas Watch representative visited Chirilagua in March 1986 to learn about mining and other wartime conditions in the area. FMLN forces have come through the town repeatedly, and occupied it between September 1983 and early 1984.

According to everyone interviewed, the guerrillas warned the population that they had mined the Alcaldía, or mayor's office, which is deserted except for soldiers' use of it as a command post when they come to town. (The building was the site of the death squad assassination of the Christian Democratic mayor in 1980.) Children sometimes play in the building, and once set off a mine by throwing rocks at it. The guerrillas later chastised them for the act.

On November 19, 1985 a soldier was killed by a guerrilla mine placed in the Alcaldía. On December 3, another soldier was wounded by a mine in the same place. He had been informed there was a mine in the building, and was searching for it in the ceiling when it exploded, blowing off his arm.

There is also mining in nearby Guadalupe, though local residents do not always agree as to which side is the source. One person we interviewed from an outlying area said that the guerrillas warn residents three days before mining, and then advise them after the mines have been removed. Some people do not believe the warnings. Another source said that the mines were placed where the Army passed, but that people had not been warned that they were there. (The guerrillas blame these mines on the Army.)

Residents reported that the area around Guadalupe has had a number of mining incidents over the past year. In November 1985, a 20-year-old man with the last name of Arévalo was walking through a field with a cow. He stepped on a mine and lost both legs, but neighbors evacuated him in a hammock to medical care in time to save his life.

On December 10, 1985, a horse stepped on a mine and its rider lost an eye. A local resident who knew the man said that he knew the area was mined, but had gone in to try, unsuccessfully, to save his horse.

We interviewed a third victim from his hospital bed. The 33-year-old man was hunting an hour's walk from Guadalupe in July 1986, when he stepped on a mine. He didn't know who placed the mine; there was no military post nearby, but both the military and the FMLN pass through. When the guerrillas mine an area, he said, they prohibit entrance.

The area where he was injured was remote, and he had to walk for an hour to get help. The ICRC brought him to a hospital on August 8, some two weeks after the injury.

The explosion removed most of the flesh from the inside part of his lower right arm, costing him his little finger. He received extensive shrapnel wounds in the chest and face, and the vision in one eye is impaired (he obviously saved himself from worse facial injury by shielding his face with his raised right arm). There were also shrapnel wounds on his left upper thigh and his right leg below the knee. He did not lose any limbs. His throat remained swollen weeks after the explosion, and when we saw him he could barely talk, although the doctors told him that his vocal cords would eventually return to normal. He told us that he thought he'd be "*mejor muerto*" -- better off dead.

Maria Armina Ascencio Valle, a 12-year-old mining victim, was born in Guadalupe and lived with her family in Chirilagua. We interviewed her in San Miguel Hospital.

Ascencio had gone with her mother and two younger siblings to collect firewood in a rural area outside Chirilagua on May 23, 1986, when she stepped on a mine. She lost her left foot in the explosion. Her brother came with a hammock to carry her to Chirilagua, and the priest drove her to the military hospital in San Miguel. A U.S. Embassy official has reported plans to have Ascencio and another young mining victim fitted with prostheses at the military hospital in San Salvador, a service that is usually unavailable to civilians.

She and others from her community had frequently gone to

the spot where the mine was laid for firewood; there had not been any previous mining incidents, and no one had been warned it was mined. Ascencio did not know who left the mine, although she guessed it was the guerrillas, since the military did not have a post in the vicinity. We were not able to ascertain the exact location of the mine, and neither she nor anyone else in the area appeared to have recent information on the guerrilla presence in the area; she said that the guerrillas used to come through "some time ago."

### El Coco, Cuscatlán

In Rosales Hospital, San Salvador, we interviewed José Gilberto Chico Pérez, 30. Chico, a tractor driver, stepped on a mine on August 15, 1986, at the turnoff to El Coco on the Aguilares-Suchitoto road. He lost his left foot in the explosion. The area where the mine was planted, on the slopes of the Guazapa volcano in the department of Cuscatlán, was recently under the control of the FMLN, and no civilians have lived there for some time. After Operation Fénix was begun in January 1986, the government declared that the area was free of guerrillas and announced plans to have civilians move back in to farm. Government spokesmen also stated that the Aguilares-Suchitoto road, closed for years by the FMLN, would be open for traffic.

At the time the mining incident took place, El Coco was still uninhabited. Some former residents -- Chico estimated 50 to 100 -- had begun to return during the day to farm, returning to Aguilares at night to live. There were several Army checkpoints on the Aguilares-Suchitoto road, and Chico considered the area

35

to be still conflictive. Shortly before the turnoff, he passed a military checkpoint in the form of a trench protected by stones, containing a tent, manned by five or six soldiers. Chico stated that they were always there when he passed through, and he had occasionally seen them patrolling in El Coco.

Chico had been hired to drive a tractor for a local farmer, who was riding along with him. They turned off the main road to head towards El Coco, the first vehicle to travel that road that day; after travelling about a block south of the turn-off, they heard a sound like a gunshot. Chico got down from the tractor to see if there was any damage. Apparently the sound had been the tractor detonating a small mine. Chico advanced a few steps in front of the tractor and stepped on the second mine. Soldiers came running down the road from the checkpoint and told him that guerrillas had probably come through during the night and mined the road. (The soldiers manned the checkpoint only by day.)

In addition to losing his left foot from mid-leg down, Chico's right foot was broken and he received shrapnel wounds in his left cheek and on his left arm. He was in traction when we saw him, and the doctors had told him that they could save his right foot.

"Who placed the mine?" we asked him. "*Los muchachos,*" he sighed, using the term commonly applied to the FMLN. He recalled a mining incident on the Aguilares-Suchitoto road itself about four months previously, in which five people died.

Chico believed the area could be dangerous because the guerrillas were still active and the Armed Forces had only recently taken it back. That is why people did not stay overnight. There had been no specific warning that this area would be mined, and

36

he himself had worked there before without incident.

### Calaboza, Usulután

Maria Angeles Cruz Arévalo, 28, was carrying plantanos when she stepped on a mine on a path in Calaboza near Zamuria, Usulután, on October 8, 1986, and lost her left foot. She is the single mother of three small children and lives in the nearby *caserio* (hamlet) Las Flores.

She went to the area with two sisters and four men. This is an area where people frequently went to gather food.

She said that they were not aware that there were any mines there and that there was no notice or warning of the mining. Although many nearby areas had been placed off limits by the FMLN, this one had not been, and people came there, to the shores near the mangroves, to gather blue crabs (*sacar punche*).

This is one of the clearest-cut cases of FMLN responsibility for mining. After the mine was detonated, the boys (FMLN) rushed up and asked her what she was doing there. She did not answer and they told her companions that they should get her out of there quickly because the soldiers were about to arrive. Her friends took her in a hammock to Ringlera (where there is a military post) and she was taken in a helicopter from there to the Sixth Brigade, and from there to the Usulután hospital.

From this, it appears that the FMLN had planted the mine for an approaching military patrol but did not warn the civilians to stay away.

The FMLN told her friends that they should not return to that area. They said that although it was not off limits (*prohibido*) before, it would be now.

## Booby-traps

The only specific example of guerrilla booby-traps we learned of first-hand came from the injured Army explosives expert. He reported finding an FMLN mine in a plastic pitcher near the township 14 de Julio in Usulután, in August 1985. The area has been abandoned for some time and remains very conflictive. The mine was detonated by the Armed Forces without any injuries. This was the only example he could recall of a booby trap, although we pressed him on this point.

## Hand-detonated Mines Resulting in Civilian Injuries

The FMLN's use of hand-detonated mines appears to be very limited. We received reports of two hand-detonated mines in which civilians travelling with military personnel were killed.

On November 5, 1985, Andrés Campos, 46, was pressured by soldiers to give them a lift in his truck as he drove along the Littoral highway in southern San Miguel. The guerrillas had warned civilians not to give soldiers rides. On a stretch of highway between El Castaño and Capulín, the guerrillas detonated a mine by remote control. It exploded under the cab of the truck (instead of the back, where the soldiers were riding). Campos was killed instantly. The Army declined to help his family with the funeral expenses.

A second incident occurred on November 17, when a salt salesman driving a truck with his wife and child as passengers gave a ride to soldiers in southern San Miguel. Guerrillas detonated a mine under the truck near the cemetery on the road

38

from El Cuco to Chirilagua. The driver was killed and his wife and child wounded.

Because these episodes involve attempts to attack soldiers, it may be that the civilian casualties should be considered collateral consequences of combat. This is particularly true in the case in which the guerrillas apparently warned civilians not to give rides to soldiers. Even if this death should not be classified as an abuse, it points up the responsibility of the FMLN to try to avoid civilian casualties as the civilian driver was the only person killed. It also points up the responsibility of the Armed Forces not to coerce civilians to undertake such hazardous tasks.

### Armed Forces Mining Practices and Violations

High-ranking officers in the Armed Forces admit only to defensive mining, such as that used around fixed installations like military bases and dams, or mining used by foot patrols to protect the perimeters of their temporary camps and outposts at night from FMLN attacks.

But a young wounded soldier interviewed by Americas Watch gave a detailed description of the Armed Forces' offensive use of land mines. This soldier, who was encountered by chance in a military hospital, was specially trained in explosives and responsible for placing a number of mines for a period of about a year prior to his injury in July 1986.[8]

The young soldier told us that the Armed Forces have used mines in ambushes and in areas where FMLN forces may camp or pass through. The unit commander decides where to mine, based on defensive needs, military intelligence, and planned operations such as ambushes and other modes of attack. The

39

injured expert told us that the Armed Forces do not leave fields mined the way the FMLN does. Mines are removed after each operation and saved for reuse, primarily as a security measure; some other Armed Forces unit could pass and set off the mines, or FMLN personnel could find the mines, deactivate them, and reuse them.

The soldier said that he laid mines at the instructions of the unit commander, informed the commander when he had done so, and kept track of the mines he laid in a notebook he carried with him. On rare occasions, he stated, the soldiers left mines in zones where no civilians transit. He emphasized that they did not leave mines where civilians pass by, and as far as he knew, none of the mines he had laid had affected civilians.

From a practical point of view, we believe that it is impossible for the Armed Forces to remove every mine they lay. Some operations are unsuccessful, and afterwards the Armed Forces do not control the territory they have mined. In other cases, the Armed Forces are unlikely to remove mines they have placed in a spot where they believe the FMLN will camp. If the guerrillas do camp at the location without detonating any or all of the mines, do Armed Forces personnel return days later to remove the mines? How do they know that the FMLN has left remote locations so they can remove the mines promptly?

Americas Watch has found no evidence to indicate that the Armed Forces deliberately target civilians in their placement of mines. Nevertheless, accidental civilian injuries can still occur. The Armed Forces are not always aware of a civilian presence in a given area, especially in a zone controlled by the FMLN, because fearful civilians may hide when the Army comes through.

Another problem in assessing the Armed Forces' claim that no civilians are injured by their mines lies in their definition of "civilian." Americas Watch uses this term interchangeably with "noncombatant," to include the residents of zones of persistence, unarmed supporters and family members of the FMLN that the guerrillas, and now the Armed Forces and the U.S. State Department, call "*masas.*" The Armed Forces tend to regard these people as a special category, and not eligible for the protection accorded to civilians. (There has been some improvement in the treatment of these people over the past two years, and no large massacres have been reported; abuses against them persist, however.)

In August 1986, for example, an official from the Joint Chiefs of Staff told us that there were no civilians living in the San Antonio area of western Cabañas. In that same month we interviewed credible witnesses who recently came from that area and who told us that there were still a number of unarmed civilians living there, many of them elderly and in poor health but too afraid of the Army to leave. Three of them were killed in a bombing in July. Either the Joint Chiefs of Staff are inadequately informed on this point, or they are intentionally continuing to jeopardize the physical security of these noncombatants by mining and bombing the area.

**Types of Mines**

The Salvadoran Armed Forces use both hand-detonated and contact mines (although the Joint Chiefs of Staff claim that only hand-detonated mines are used). All of the mines have the capacity to injure, and some of them can kill.

The Army issues two types of mines of U.S. manufacture, the Claymore M-14 and M-18. The M-14, which can be detonated by hand or by contact, is considered to be an anti-personnel weapon, while the more powerful M-18, which is described as exclusively hand-detonated, is an anti-vehicle or anti-tank weapon. U.S. Embassy sources state that the only mine the U.S. provides to the Armed Forces is the M-18.

The injured explosives expert told Americas Watch representatives that in addition to Claymore mines, the Armed Forces also use grenades and "homemade" mines of the same sort the FMLN has, describing their practices in convincing detail (again contradicting a high army official, who told us that the Armed Forces use only Claymores).

The grenades, which are of U.S. manufacture, are converted into contact mines by removing the pin and inserting a branch or other stopper. When a passer-by hits the branch, the mine explodes. These devices are usually used to guard the perimeter of temporary camps. To remove the mine, a soldier must carefully reinsert the pin while removing the branch. We know of at least one incident this year in which a soldier was assigned to deactivate the mines surrounding a temporary camp, apparently performed the task carelessly, and was killed immediately as a result. The Army's contact mines are of the same basic designs as those used by the FMLN.

The Army frequently creates mines out of grenades set with trip wires, according to a 27-year-old wounded guerrilla combatant from Guazapa interviewed this year. The Army uses small grenades as well as grenades fired from grenade launchers, which the wounded guerrilla called "the 81 mortar" and "the 120 cannon." Although he estimates that the Army has used these mines since 1983, he himself has seen few mining accidents. He added that the Army has stepped up its use of mines since Operation Fénix (a sustained effort to dislodge both guerrillas and *masas* from Guazapa and other "zones of persistence") began in January 1986. He described one Army mine dismantled by the FMLN in May 1986 in a deserted canton frequented by civilians from Suchitoto (who go in search of fruit and firewood). The mine, he said, was made of three grenades set to be triggered by a wire stretched across the path. He deactivated a similar mine, made up of two grenades, near the San Martín-Suchitoto highway in September 1985.

According to an article by Chris Hedges in *The Dallas Morning News*, an Army official has admitted that he has ordered the relocation of FMLN mines, which would make the Army, not the FMLN, responsible for resulting injuries:

> "We use mines at night to defend our positions," said Col. Miguel Alfredo Vasconcelos, the commander of the Sixth Brigade in Usulután, one of the hardest hit by rebel mining. "In the morning these mines are all collected."
>
> The Colonel admitted that they occasionally transplanted rebel mines in mountainous areas dominated by the guerrillas.
>
> "The guerrillas use mines in southern Usulután to protect their supply routes," the Colonel said. "Sometimes these routes are several kilometers wide. They also use mines to protect their camps. If we find mines around their positions we will sometimes move them to disrupt the guerrilla patrols once they

43

return, but we do not transplant mines if there are civilians living near by." (*The Dallas Morning News,* August 10, 1986.

The Army does not reuse FMLN mines in every region, however. The wounded expert we interviewed said that his detachments activated FMLN mines instead of saving them for reuse because they were unsure of their contents, and wanted to avoid mine handlers' injuries from the devices going off accidentally.

Given that the Armed Forces do replant FMLN mines on some occasions, and that they also use improvised mines similar to those of the FMLN, there is public confusion in a number of cases as to which side is responsible for placing a given homemade mine. FMLN combatants have accused the Army of leaving mines and blaming the FMLN for the resulting injuries in the attempt to discredit them, although these charges cannot be substantiated.

### Guidelines for Use

The Armed Forces' use of Claymore mines is governed by instructions issued in 1985 by General Adolfo O. Blandón, head of the Joint Chiefs of Staff, in preparation for the distribution of those mines.

The instructions, labelled "secret" and provided to us by the Joint Chiefs of Staff, state that the Claymore mines will be distributed only to the units that have been specially trained in their use. Only manual detonation is permitted, and the "zone of death" should be in clear view to the troops, both before and after the detonation.

Before detonating a mine, the unit using it should assure that the objective is enemy personnel and not civilians. The mines may be used in defensive positions, including in cities, if the zone is clearly marked as "mined." Mines should be removed when troops leave a defensive position, patrol base, or locale of ambush.

These instructions are in keeping with desired standards in some respects, but they are limited to the use of Claymores, lack detail about security measures, and make no provisions for recording the location of mines.

Furthermore, even these instructions are not followed to the letter. In our interview with the injured explosives expert, he said that the M-14 mines were left in areas the guerrillas frequented or used as operational bases, according to military intelligence. Army personnel bury the M-14s in such locations, leaving the switch in the active position so that pressure of even 20 or 30 pounds will activate it. Its effect is to maim; it is small and is likely to blow off the feet of the person who steps on it (as its nickname, "*quitapata*," indicates), like the homemade guerrilla mines we have criticized in the accompanying section. In the usage described to us, the Army's M-14 mines are not hand-detonated. This is clearly a violation of the guidelines issued by the Joint Chiefs of Staff.

There are no Armed Forces guidelines for using or removing mines other than Claymores, such as the improvised mines and grenades. We were told by officials from the Joint Chiefs of Staff that no written instructions for the use of mines exist beyond the two-page document governing Claymores we were given.

## Case Studies of Armed Forces Mining

In the first six months of 1986, investigations by the human rights office of the Catholic Church, Tutela Legal, showed that there were three deaths from Armed Forces mines.

Manuel Orlando Melara, 54, died from a military mine placed inside the cotton cooperative Entre Rios, canton El Socorro, in the zone of Zacatecoluca, on February 15, 1986. The U.S. Embassy mining tally agrees that this mine was placed by Armed Forces personnel who, the Embassy indicated, were mining the cooperative to protect it from guerrilla attacks. (The government Human Rights Commission lists it as a guerrilla mine, as do the Armed Forces.) Apparently the Armed Forces did not adequately warn the cooperative members that the area was mined.

### Morazán

Tutela Legal lists two additional mining deaths in April 1986 as the responsibility of the Armed Forces, though the tallies of government-related institutions do not agree. Both incidents occurred in Osicala, Morazán on April 18, 1986. Marcial Vásquez, age unknown, died after he stepped on an Armed Forces mine at the turnoff to Osicala. Ramón García, 40, died around 6 a.m. the same day after stepping on a defensive mine laid by the Second Company of support from the Morazán Battalion in the San Rafael neighborhood of Osicala.

It appears that these three mines were laid in a manner that violated Armed Forces guidelines for the laying of Claymore mines, since they were not hand detonated and they were placed in areas where civilians transit, which were not areas under the control of the FMLN. We do not know if the mines were Claymore mines.

### Cabañas

Two other testimonies recently taken by Tutela Legal state that the Armed Forces located a number of mines in the FMLN-controlled zone of western Cabañas in 1985. One mine killed the declarant's nephew, Ursulo Moso López, 16, as he travelled from San Antonio, Cabañas, to Tenancingo, Cuscatlán, in March 1985.

In the second testimony, a refugee reports:

> In September 1985, after an Army operation in the Canton La Criba [between Jutiapa and Cinquera in Cabañas] the soldiers left mines. I was fleeing, I was in front and the others behind, and we were on the path where the soldiers had passed, and then I stepped on an explosive and that was where I was wounded in the lower leg. I still have the scar in the lower leg. I was the only one hurt, because by luck the other people, including a lot of children, were behind me. It took me two or three months to recover. The soldiers always leave the field mined when they go.

This last statement, if true, directly contradicts claims that the Armed Forces only rarely leave mines behind, and then only in areas where civilians do not transit.

There have been repeated instances of mining incidents following Army sweeps, the evidence suggesting that the soldiers leave the mines behind. One such incident took place in November 1985. Bernabé Hernández, 40, had fled an eight-day Army sweep through his home town of San Antonio, Cabañas, along with other civilians from the zone. He went back to recover bananas that he had hidden from the Army. As he left his house to walk to the banana grove, he set off a mine, perhaps by tripping a wire, and died two hours later. One witness who viewed his body stated that large pieces of his legs were missing.

The same witness noted that she spotted another mine in January 1986 during Operation Fénix. The mine, which was placed at the foot of a tree, was olive green, about one-and-a-half feet in diameter and about eight inches deep. It was obviously not homemade, and was probably a Claymore. She and others saw the mine about 5 p.m. and went to advise others of it. When someone went to deactivate it at 6 a.m. the next morning, it had been moved, presumably by soldiers. No one was hurt. Parachute troops had left eight mines behind in a neighboring hamlet called El Filo in February 1985.

One 21-year-old FMLN combatant from the Cabañas region said that FMLN forces deactivated a number of mines near Tenango in early 1986 when there were still about 50 civilians in residence. Only one of the mines actually exploded, killing the dog that stepped on it; there were no civilian casualties.

# NICARAGUA

The land mines that have caused civilian casualties in Nicaragua have been planted primarily on roads in the north. These roads are used by civilian as well as military vehicles, and serve as the only means of travel and commerce between the towns of the area. With the exception of the Rio Coco area of the Atlantic Coast, the use of mines has not yet spread into the rest of the country; the most affected zone continues to be Region 6 (Matagalpa and Jinotega). The heaviest concentration of mines has been found in and around the communities of El Cuá, Bocay, Wiwilí, El Carmen, and Pantasma/Sompopera.

Region 6 has been the hardest hit: from March until October 1986, its population suffered at least 45 civilian deaths and an additional number of injuries due to land mines, according to international press reports, military officials and nongovernmental international organizations that monitor such events.

Unlike El Salvador, multiple sources of nationwide statistics are not available; we are aware of only a single source. In September 1986, prior to an October 20 episode in which 6 civilians were killed and 30 civilians were wounded (see below) the Nicaraguan government's human rights commission (CNPPDH) informed Americas Watch that it had tabulated 25 civilian deaths and 12 civilian woundings due to mines in 1985; and 49 civilian deaths and 20 civilian woundings due to mines in 1986. CNPPDH also said that it had tabulated 7 Sandinista soldiers killed and 27 wounded in 1985; and 22 Sandinista soldiers killed and 38 wounded in 1986. Americas Watch has not independently verified these figures but the number of civilian deaths seems consistent with the number reported by foreign journalists, while the number of civilian woundings and the number of soldiers killed and wounded seem understated. The non-governmental domestic human rights organization in Nicaragua, CPDH, does not attempt to gather data on such matters.

There is no real debate as to who is laying the mines that are killing and injuring civilians in Nicaragua: it is the anti-Sandinista rebel forces, or *contras*. (See below for a description of episodes that have taken place across the border in Honduras that are apparently attributable to Nicaraguan government mining.) The mines are placed on main roads that are used by Nicaraguan government army vehicles for troop and supply transport, among other needs. These mines have been well inside the areas under government control, and do not perform a defensive function for any *contra* activities or controlled zones in Nicaragua. Indeed, most nongovernment, and non-*contra*, observers say that the *contras* do not control territory inside Nicaragua (unlike the FMLN in El Salvador).

It should be noted that the *contras* themselves do not acknowledge their use of mines. A spokesman for the United Nicaraguan Opposition (UNO), the group through which the U.S.

funds the *contras*, and for the Nicaraguan Democratic Force (FDN), the principal combatant organization, told Americas Watch in November that forces allied with UNO do not use mines. The spokesman said those forces previously used only remote controlled Claymore mines, but that these have not been used for more than two years. When they were used, he said, it was exclusively against military units. He further told Americas Watch that the Sandinista forces used mines extensively in Nicaragua, and that these mines are known as "supras," they are the same as those used by the FMLN in El Salvador; that they are believed to be of Soviet origin; that they are designed to mutilate; and that they are the same kind of mine that was used to kill two U.S. journalists in Honduras in 1983. Except for the attribution of the deaths of the two journalists to Nicaraguan government mining, these assertions are contradicted in every particular by the evidence that we have been able to gather from other sources. That evidence supports the view that mining that causes civilian casualties inside Nicaragua is attributable to the *contras*.

According to our interviews with injured civilians, the *contras* have made no effort to warn the civilian population of the placement of mines. Even if the mines are intended for military vehicles, they often strike civilian targets because they are contact mines, they are placed on main highways that serve as essential routes for civilians, and civilians use the mined roads more frequently than the military does. The civilian deaths are directly foreseeable and avoidable, but the *contras* take no precautions to avoid civilian casualties.

The *contras* apparently take the position in practice that the Sandinista army has "militarized" various regions, thus legitimizing attacks on any vehicles within these regions. It is an argument that the U.S. State Department has used on several occasions to justify *contra* attacks on farming cooperatives, such as an attack on a cooperative at Comoapa in June 1986 in which the victims included a number of children. This argument fails to exercise the discrimination required of combatants in distinguishing between military and nonmilitary targets on a case-by-case basis, and taking the proper precautions to avoid noncombatant injury and death.

*The New York Times* described the military significance of mines in the two northern regions in an article by Stephen Kinzer published July 19:

> Government soldiers interviewed at several outposts said they had lost comrades when blasts tore through troop transport trucks.
>
> Land mines are reported to have destroyed trucks on all three of the rugged dirt roads that spread north from the provincial capital [of Jinotega]. Twisted wrecks of vehicles are visible near the roads in several places.
>
> The roads, strewn with rocks and at times impassable, are vital to both the Sandinista army and the thousands of peasants who live in this poor agricultural zone.
>
> For the rebels, mining the roads would allow them to strike against concentrated groups of Government troops without risking firefights.

A Nicaraguan Joint Chiefs of Staff official stationed in

Military Region 6 (which includes Region 6 plus some additional territory) said that his forces began to find *contra* mines in the zone in February or March 1985. The mines caused some civilian casualties, and were then apparently suspended for a year. *Contra* mining in that area began again in March 1986 and continues today. The official said that the mining appeared to be stepped up in conjunction with the *contra* offensive planned for Estelí's July 19th celebration (the anniversary of the 1979 Sandinista takeover); the offensive itself did not materialize.

On July 19, *The New York Times* reported that:

> According to diplomats who see Western intelligence data, the rebels, known as *contras*, began buying large numbers of mines in the second half of 1985. "The *contras* have gone into mines in a big way," said one diplomat who has received intelligence reports from Jinotega.

One well-informed source told us that there is little doubt the roads were mined by the *contras*. Nonetheless, he believes the *contras* have no elaborated policy on mining, and began to deploy mines on a haphazard basis, perhaps after acquiring some on the international arms market. He also expects their use to escalate, due to their modest cost in money and manpower, and their utility towards achieving major *contra* objectives, such as cutting off a major artery like the road to Rama.

Sandinista army personnel say that the *contras'* objective is to impede circulation of traffic, destroy the economy, and cause terror among the population. They believe that the *contras* act out of frustration because of their lack of military success.

It is uncertain whether those are the *contras'* objectives, or whether they simply want to attack military vehicles and are reckless in their placement of the mines. What is clear is that the mines are highly effective militarily, although at great cost to civilians.

The people who lay the mines are well-trained, according to Sandinista army spokesmen, who believe that the *contras* leave the mines in the houses of their civilian supporters in the area, then come by for them and lay them at night.

One additional important factor in the question of land mines has been Misura, the largely Miskito insurgent force operating on the Atlantic Coast, now known as Kisan. On a trip from Puerto Cabezas to the Rio Coco in January 1986, an Americas Watch representative saw the wrecks of several military trucks by the side of the road. Civilians familiar with the area said that Misura mined the road on several occasions and blew up the trucks. Misura was also responsible for a mine that killed five civilians whose place of death is commemorated by five white crosses beside the main road from Puerto Cabezas to Waspam on the Rio Coco.

A former Misura/Kisan combatant -- now a member of Kisan Pro Paz -- interviewed by Americas Watch in July 1986 said that Misura/Kisan used remote-controlled mines and contact mines, frequently Claymore antitank mines. He told us that they put them in the roads where only military vehicles pass, offering the examples of the roads to Waspam, Tronquera, and Bismona. However, these roads also carry civilian traffic.

## Types of Mines Used by the Contras

Army officials at the headquarters of Military Region 6 in Matagalpa showed Americas Watch representatives two mines, or parts of mines, stating that they had been laid by the *contras* and detected and deactivated by Sandinista forces. One mine was labeled TM-72-M. The Sandinistas did not know the country of origin; it could be Brazil or Czechoslovakia. It weighs 10 kilos when fully assembled (we were not shown the entire device) and functions as a contact mine that explodes with pressure of 150 kilos or more. It is capable of destroying a four-ton vehicle.

Another local military official agreed that this kind of mine was introduced in the region in 1986. The first one found in the Abisinia area of Jinotega caused the explosion in La Pita in July (discussed below), in which a civilian vehicle was struck and a woman passenger killed.

The second type of mine used by the *contras* is the Claymore M 18 A1 -- the same kind the U.S. Army provides to the Salvadoran Army. We saw a piece of an M 18; on the section labeled "BACK" it said:

M 18 A1 APERS MINE
LOT LOP-13-23 9-75
FRONT TOWARDS ENEMY

The back also contained the message: "Warning. Explosive is poisonous if eaten. Do not Burn. Produces toxic gases."

The back was concave, the front convex. There were two telescopic legs that extended from the mine, enabling the soldier to place it in the ground. A hand device was squeezed to

55

detonate the mine, the signal passing through a connecting cord. The M 18 was introduced by the *contras* in Nicaragua around 1983, but Sandinista officials state that it is not widely used.

The third type of mine used by the *contras* is the Brazilian antipersonnel mine. It is a small, light contact mine that requires only three pounds of pressure to explode; it injures but rarely kills. The *contras* first used them in 1986. Sandinista officials say that eleven of their soldiers have been injured by these mines in the sixth region this year, with no fatalities. (These figures seem far too low, but we have no independent source with which to dispute them.) The mines are laid on paths where the Army patrols, not on major roads.

This antipersonnel mine has the nickname "*quitadedos*," or "removes toes." A local official told us that eight Sandinista soldiers had been wounded by this type of mine in the Abisinia area between May and July 1986. In August 1985, a civilian from the town of Monte Cristo was wounded by one when he was cutting underbrush to clear a field.

## Civilian Casualties

On September 2, 1986, Americas Watch interviewed a civilian government representative in Matagalpa who estimated that of the 30 antitank mines found in Region 6 in 1986, 12 had exploded and 18 had been deactivated. Half of the exploded mines injured civilians.

We have compiled a list of seven mining incidents affecting civilians in Military Region 6. in which 42 civilians were killed and 45 injured between May 17 and October 20, 1986. (An eighth incident has been excluded from this calculation by

Americas Watch because it appears that the victims may have been armed and/or uniformed members of the FSLN.) Of the seven incidents, survivors of three have been interviewed by Americas Watch; a fourth incident, in which 34 people died, was covered by several journalists.

**Military Casualties**

Sandinista military authorities would not confirm or deny the number of military vehicles that have struck land mines.[9] An official from Military Region 6 told us that more civilians than military were killed by mines; according to the list he gave us (we recognize, of course, the difficulty in reconciling these figures with others we have obtained), and counting FSLN victims who may have been armed, 46 civilians died and 18 were injured by mines from March through August 1986. The official said that 21 soldiers were killed and 12 were wounded in Military Region 6 during the same period. This information, however, has been contradicted by other sources, including a lower-ranking military man who said that about 30 soldiers were killed by a mine that blew up a truck. In addition, an officer on duty outside the military hospital in Apanas interviewed by *The New York Times* in July said that about 25 Sandinista soldiers were recovering in the special hospital unit for mining victims. He said most of the land-mine victims he knew of had died at the scene of the explosion.

## Case Studies of Contra Mining

### El Cedro, Jinotega

On July 2, 1986, 34 civilians were killed by a mining incident on the main road in San Juan del Bocay, near the Honduran border. Eighteen of the victims were members of one extended family that had been relocated from their town near Bocay because of the war.

The only survivor was a man who was one of the last to get on the truck. He had been riding on the rear bumper, hanging off the end. The blast knocked him into a tree a long distance away, burning his left arm and breaking several ribs. The man was left unconscious for up to half an hour, when local residents passed by and called the Army.

According to an article about the incident by Bill Gasperini written on July 16 and published in *In These Times*:

> Since early May, 35 other civilians have died in at least 5 mine blasts. On May 24, a mine killed nine people on the same road, including a popular Spanish health worker....
>
> Combined with the explosion of a reserve barrel of gas in the truck, commonly carried by vehicles in the remote region, the blast incinerated the bodies beyond recognition and blackened the forest around the narrow dirt road. Two cadavers were so dismembered that it took several days to piece them together, raising the original death toll from 32 to 34, while one person miraculously survived.

58

The incident made more of an impact after reports surfaced in some major newspapers questioning the government's account of the incident. *The New York Times* even suggested the mine could have been placed by the Sandinistas, basing that assessment on anonymous comments from diplomats in Managua. [A subsequent *New York Times* article made it clear that the mine had been placed by the *contras*.] Others speculated that the civilians died when the gas barrel exploded and not from the mine.

"There is no possibility the gas explosion could have killed all those people," said Fred Depenbrock, member of a Witness for Peace delegation which also inspected the site. "The blast only ripped the top off the barrel, while the whole back left side of the truck was missing." The burning gasoline apparently finished off those not killed in the immediate detonation.

A U.S. reserve combat engineer with experience in mine warfare also on the delegation said the mine could have been a U.S.-made M-15, judging from the size of the crater and the remains of the truck. Such devices contain 25 pounds of explosives designed to rip through armored metal such as a tank. In normal combat situations soldiers prepare minefields with the devices to prevent enemy troops from advancing....

"They want to terrorize us and prevent food from arriving," said Bocay resident Virginia Esquivel (75), "Before people would bring in sugar, soap and other provisions, but who will come now?" Two of the victims were merchants bringing market items from Jinotega, the closest city 80 miles away.

The vehicle that hit the mine was a nonmilitary and nongovernment truck that was making a regular delivery of supplies to Bocay. As is the custom in rural areas, the driver had given a ride to the 34 people who were in the truck when it ran over the mine. There were no soldiers on the truck.

According to witnesses who talked to the driver shortly before his death, he had been warned a few days earlier by men on the road, whom he took to be *contras*, to stop making deliveries to Bocay. There was no mention of mining.

The mine was placed on the only access road to a town of 1500 -- not on the nearby road to the military base. It was inevitable that civilian vehicles would pass over the road, despite the danger from the *contras*, because the civilians in the town and outlying hamlets depend on commerce and transportation by truck to survive.

It should be noted that The White House, in an October 15, 1986 report to Congress, attempted to cast doubt on the accounts of this episode that were published in the U.S. press. The White House ignored the visits to the site by U.S. journalists, and attempted to make it appear that all accounts of the mining stemmed from Sandinista sources. Its report to Congress said:

On July 3, the official Nicaraguan press reported that a civilian truck had struck a mine emplaced by the resistance, resulting in the deaths of 32 civilians. Simultaneously with the Sandinista report, resistance headquarters was informed that a grenade thrown at a

60

resistance unit by Sandinista forces had hit a passing truck, causing an explosion that resulted in the deaths of thirty-one civilians, including an evangelical pastor. There is no evidence available to confirm either version of events.

The information gathered at the scene by independent observers, and the effort to attribute the report of the mining solely to Sandinista sources, make it plain that The White House's effort to shift responsibility is ludicrous.

This was the only mention of mining by either side in The White House's twenty-page report to Congress on Nicaragua.

### The Road from Wiwilí to Jinotega

On June 11, 1986, a mine exploded under a civilian truck carrying 15 passengers, all civilians, on the main road from Wiwilí to Jinotega, resulting in a number of injuries and one (unconfirmed) death. Americas Watch interviewed the owner of the truck, Audilio René Montenegro, 39, on August 7, 1986 at his home in Jinotega.

The road where the incident took place is the only road between Wiwilí and Jinotega, and is frequented by civilian traffic as well as military vehicles. Montenegro had left Wiwilí early that morning. Before his departure, he checked with the authorities, who had been prohibiting traffic on the road when they believed it to be unsafe. On the morning of the 11th, they "guaranteed" the road as far as Pantasma. There had been mines on that road earlier; Montenegro had heard of one hitting a Housing Ministry vehicle in early June, killing several civilians.

Three people, including Montenegro, were riding in the cab, and another 15 passengers stood in the back of the truck. It had been raining, and the truck swerved a fair amount to avoid rough patches in the road. At about 10 a.m. the truck ran over and detonated a mine that was in a pothole covered with water in the middle of the road. It exploded under the back right wheel, throwing the truck into the air; it reportedly landed 30 meters ahead. Montenegro, shaken but unhurt, believed as the others did that they had driven into a *contra* ambush.

The worst casualty appeared to be a woman passenger who was wounded in the feet, face, and eyes. Montenegro was told that she died later in the hospital, but he is not certain. A boy standing near her got a fractured foot. Shortly after the explosion, someone came and took the passengers, nearly all of whom sustained some kind of injury from the expansive wave of the mine, to the health center at Pantasma.

Montenegro said he had been warned off that route by the *contras* three years ago and told he was not to use the road or they would burn his truck. He received no warnings after that. Other truckers were warned by the *contras*, but never regarding mines.

### La Pita del Carmen, Jinotega

On June 17, 1986, a civilian truck ran over and detonated a Claymore antitank mine on a side road near La Pita del Carmen, killing a passenger and injuring the driver. Americas Watch interviewed the driver in his Jinotega home on August 8, 1986. He had lost his right foot in the blast and sustained injuries on both arms, his face, and stomach. He was on crutches, awaiting an artificial limb. (He was told he could not go abroad to be fitted with a prosthetic device because he was not a member of the military, but the state cattle enterprise where he worked has promised to provide him with one within four months.)

The explosion occurred when the driver's civilian truck ran over an antitank mine. A woman, Manuela Ubeda de Casco, 60, was riding with him in the front seat. She was killed and he was told that only the upper half of her body was recovered. The driver was unconscious for nine days. His teen-aged helper, riding in the back, was thrown from the truck and escaped without injury. All three were unarmed civilians; there were no other passengers.

The road where the incident took place was cleared about three years ago, a narrow, mountainous path with room for only one car at a time. The road passes by a few houses and farmland, but does not go by any military installations. The driver took this road because he was buying bananas for someone and had to go down this road to pick them up. He had not traveled the road for the previous year. The *contras* passed through the area frequently, but he had never been stopped by them or warned by them.

A military official in Abisinia, however, told Americas Watch that the road had not been used by the military for a while because of the mine problem. Usually the army patrols the road with a metal detector, but because of the constant *contra* presence in the vicinity, they had decided not to use the road for the preceding two years.

### The Road from Jinotega to San José de Bocay at Bocaycito, Matagalpa

On August 3, 1986, a truck full of civilian passengers hit a mine at the edge of a stream near Bocaycito, Matagalpa, wounding 16 or 17 passengers. Americas Watch interviewed three of the victims, all women, in the hospital in Jinotega, and a fourth male victim in his home. The incident occurred on the same road where 34 civilians were killed by a mine explosion July 2 near El Cedro.

The mine exploded under a rear tire, and many of the victims were thrown from the truck. One victim who did not lose consciousness said that both tires were blown and the rear of the truck was badly damaged. She said the hole left by the mine was about a meter in circumference.

Two of the women interviewed were suffering from internal injuries caused by the expansive wave of the mine. One was thrown twenty yards or so from the vehicle and spent some fifteen minutes unconscious in the underbrush. At the time of the interview, she was still suffering pains in her body and her feet, in part from the expansive wave and in part from the fall.

A third victim suffered from the same symptoms, in addition to an injured left foot that continues to bleed; she hopes that it will not be amputated. She also received shrapnel in her right calf. She said that shortly after the explosion, the driver sent word back to Bocaycito and the military arrived. Soldiers made a brace out of branches to support her foot. She was taken to the nearest health center in the town of El Cuá, and later to the hospital in Jinotega, where she was given an injection for the pain.

64

A 50-year-old man told Americas Watch that he was riding in the back of the truck. He was thrown into the air and, he believes, landed in the river; he says that when he regained consciousness five hours later in El Cuá, he was still wet. The hospital personnel had wanted to operate on his left leg, but he refused the operation. He had multiple cuts on his face as well.

One of the female victims said that no vehicles had been allowed on the road where the incident took place on Friday or Saturday. When their truck left from San José de Bocay early Sunday morning, it was the first vehicle out. Apparently the Army had failed to detect the mine before allowing the truck to use the road or the mine was placed after any checking undertaken by the Army.

**Pantasma, Jinotega**

On October 23, James Le Moyne reported in *The New York Times*:

> At least 6 civilians were killed and 30 seriously wounded Monday [October 20] when their crowded civilian transport truck ran over a powerful land mine ... according to several wounded passengers and doctors at the scene.
>
> The attack was the second major civilian disaster in recent months caused by a land mine that area residents believe was planted by United States-backed guerrillas. A rebel official denied that the guerrillas had planted the mine.
>
> The mine blew through the bottom of the village's

65

daily civilian transport truck, hurling peasant passengers in all directions, according to 10 witnesses who were in the truck or involved in rescue efforts.

"There was blood, personal belongings and other effects scattered everywhere," said Dr. Maj G. Stormogipson, a Presbyterian church volunteer doctor who works in the region and who rushed to the scene to treat survivors....

All of the wounded are civilians, according to hospital records and survivors.

### Somotillo, Chinandega

Americas Watch's March 1986 report, "Human Rights in Nicaragua, 1985-1986," described an episode that took place on February 10, 1986. Stephen Kinzer had reported in *The New York Times* that "a land mine tore through a pickup truck carrying 17 civilians. A rebel band waiting in ambush then opened fire. Five women ranging in age from 28 to 70 were killed. A Swiss agronomist who had worked in the area for three years also died."

Americas Watch's March report also cited another account of this episode. Based on this other account, we said that "there were actually four women killed in this attack" and that "eleven women were injured, some of them seriously." Subsequently, we learned that Stephen Kinzer's account in the *Times* was correct; four women had died instantly, but one of the injured women died shortly thereafter. Americas Watch regrets the implication in our earlier report that Mr. Kinzer's account was mistaken.

With respect to this attack, the fact that a *contra* band

66

opened fire on those who had been injured by the land mine tends to suggest that the attack on civilians was deliberate.

The deaths and injuries in this February episode are not included in the May to October statistics cited above. Also, this episode took place in a different region.

## Government Mines

The government mines access to bridges throughout the country, as Americas Watch has observed in various parts of the country in 1986. These bridges are clearly marked with signs saying, "danger -- mined field -- entry prohibited;" some are also marked with a skull and cross bones. The mined areas are fenced off by posts that are five feet high with six to eight strands of barbed wire, making access impossible for children and the illiterate as well.

We are aware of one episode in which a mine near a bridge was inadequately marked and civilian casualties resulted. According to information gathered by Witness for Peace, a woman was killed and two persons were injured in early October 1986 by an explosion at Quilali, near Jinotega.

Aside from this, Sandinista military officials claim that the army uses only hand-detonated mines (inside the country) and leave the mines only in depopulated areas where they believe the *contras* will pass through.

On July 19, 1986, *The New York Times* reported:

The Sandinistas are believed to have received antitank mines from the Soviet bloc, but Western military analysts in Managua said they believed the weapons were being held back by the Sandinistas in case of an armored invasion from Honduras.

The Nicaraguan government admits to having mined stretches of the Honduran border, where the civilian population has been relocated by the government. These mines are placed in spots of possible *contra* incursions from Honduras. The military official interviewed by Americas Watch considered these areas to be mine fields and military combat zones; soldiers are posted near each one, and civilians are warned to keep out. Americas Watch has not learned of any civilian casualties inside Nicaragua that can be attributed to Nicaraguan government mining. The FDN has claimed, however, that civilians have been hurt by government mines in Nicaragua. These would probably be civilians attempting to cross the border illegally.

The other episode that we know about in which civilians were killed by a mine that probably was planted by Nicaraguan government forces occurred immediately across the border in Honduras on June 21, 1983. The victims were two American journalists, Dial Torgerson, a correspondent for *The Los Angeles Times*; and Richard Cross, a free-lance photographer. Their car passed over a mine on a road near the town of Las Trojes at a point where the road passes some 20 to 30 yards from the Nicaraguan border. The area around Las Trojes has been occupied for several years by *contra* forces that conduct raids into Nicaragua; much of the Honduran civilian population has been displaced from the area by the *contras*.

Juan Tamayo of the Knight Ridder newspapers was one of those who went to the scene after Torgerson and Cross were killed. He reported in the June 30, 1983 *Washington Post* that:

*Miami Herald* photographer Murray Sill and I first came across the mines last Thursday in the middle of the road that belongs to Honduras and is about 20 to 30 yards from the barbed-wire fence that marks the border in that sector.

Photographs taken by the [Honduran] commandos and displayed by [Honduran Colonel] Lopez Grijalva showed that the front end of the journalists' car was completely demolished....

Eight feet from the car was a round crater, three feet wide and 18 inches deep, where the mine had been buried, Lopez Grijalva said. Within a five-foot radius, the Honduran troops found two unexploded anti-tank mines and five smaller antipersonnel mines.

On July 16, 1983, *The Los Angeles Times* carried an Associated Press dispatch that quoted a State Department assessment of the deaths of Torgerson and Cross. According to the article, the State Department said that:

Although absolute proof of responsibility for this tragic incident is not now available, and may never be, the full weight of the available evidence ... leads us to the conclusion that [the journalists] ... were killed by Nicaraguan forces.

Juan Tamayo's article in *The Washington Post* of June 30, 1983 concluded with a grisly note about an injury that occurred at the time that Torgerson and Cross were killed:

69

Found near the car was the foot of a Honduran peasant who triggered a mine when he approached the wrecked car moments after it exploded, said Lopez Grijalva. The peasant, who also lost an eye, is in a Tegucigalpa hospital, he said.

None of the accounts of this 1983 episode that we have examined includes information about warnings of any kind. Given the circumstances, it appears to us that this episode should be blamed on the Nicaraguan government.

A November 11, 1986 article by Julia Preston in *The Washington Post*, "Honduras Feels Impact of Contra War," cites more recent mining by Nicaraguan government forces inside Honduras in the vicinity of Las Trojes. According to Preston:

A 14-mile stretch of heavily traveled public roadway between Las Trojes and the next town, Cifuentes, has suffered repeated Sandinista attacks in the past three months. The attacks appear aimed at halting the many truckloads of contra supplies using the road.

Preston's article goes on to report two cases in which civilians were injured by mines in this area. "Local authorities" are cited as the source for the information that a "government agronomist was severely injured in August when his vehicle struck a land mine." In the other case, Preston interviewed the victim, a farmworker named Jose Arnulfo Sosa "whose right leg was amputated after it was ripped apart Oct. 13 by a hidden mine in a coffee plantation far from the contra camps and nine miles inside Honduras." Preston quotes Sosa, a father of five, as saying "I'll never be able to work again."

Preston's article also says that "U.S. officials said several dozen civilians have been maimed or killed by the mines in the past six months," but does not provide any details about dates, places or identities of those who may have been killed. Finally, the article cites "local reports" that many Honduran soldiers have been mine victims, but points out that "The Honduran military is reluctant to divulge its casualties."

# RECOMMENDATIONS

Obviously, the ideal resolution to the problem of civilian land mine casualties in El Salvador and Nicaragua would be a voluntary decision on the part of the various parties to the conflict to suspend completely their use in areas with any civilian presence. However, the realities of warfare leave this a distant hope.

Barring such a resolution, the parties to the conflict should adopt a firm policy to provide "adequate warnings" to the civilian population in mined areas, and, on a case-by-case, region-by-region basis, decide what an "adequate warning" should be. The appropriate warnings may vary considerably, but it is the responsibility of the combatants, all of whom claim the sympathies of the civilian populations, to work out the most effective means to protect them. Depending on the area, these could involve:

1. town meetings to announce areas that are mined and off-limits.

2. posted warnings on mined paths and areas, preferably

using a universal symbol that would be comprehensible to children and illiterate adults.

3. house-to-house warnings in rural zones.

4. radio broadcasts.

In most cases, more than one method would be necessary. It is the responsibility of the parties to maintain records of their placement of mines and to remove them promptly when their military purposes have expired. Also, the parties should make their warning methods public and should cooperate with human rights groups in monitoring compliance with their own guidelines.

We call upon the parties to the conflict to discuss these suggestions and to develop others, implementing whichever measures would be most appropriate to the zone and conditions in question. Also, we call on the parties to renounce and avoid entirely the use of booby-traps, the mining of the wounded or the dead, and the mining of objects intended for civilian use.

The development of such practices could save civilian lives in Central America, and set a small but important precedent on behalf of civilians suffering the consequences of such conflicts around the globe.

# APPENDIX

## Applicability of Rules in the Land Mines Protocol to the Internal Armed Conflicts in El Salvador and Nicaragua

The principal source of international law rules governing the use of land mines and comparable explosive devices is the Protocol on Prohibitions or Restrictions on the Use of Mines, Booby Traps and Other Devices (Protocol II), annexed to the 1981 UN Convention on Prohibition or Restrictions on the Use of Certain Conventional Weapons Which May be Deemed to be Excessively Injurious and to Have Indiscriminate Effects ("UN Convention").[10]

By Article I of the UN Convention, the Land Mines Protocol applies only to interstate, i.e., international, armed conflicts as defined in Article 2[11] common to the 1949 Geneva Conventions and to a limited class of "wars of national liberation" described in paragraph 4 of Article 1 of Additional Protocol I[12] to these conventions. Since El Salvador and Nicaragua[13] have not ratified these instruments, neither state is legally bound by their terms.

And, even if both states had done so, the provisions of these instruments would still not directly apply as treaty obligations to the ongoing conflicts in both states since neither conflict meets the threshold requirement of Article 1 of the UN Convention.

As noted in previous Americas Watch reports, the present nature of the hostilities in both countries, while obviously having international political dimensions, is that of an internal, i.e., non-international armed conflict. Thus, both conflicts are governed by two sets of humanitarian law rules: those set forth in Article 3[14] common to the 1949 Geneva Conventions ("Article 3") to which both Nicaragua and El Salvador are state parties, and those customary international law rules applicable to internal armed conflicts. In the case of El Salvador, the warring parties are also bound by Protocol II additional to the 1949 Geneva Conventions.[15]

The fact that the Land Mines Protocol is not directly binding on El Salvador and Nicaragua does not mean, however, that this instrument's authoritative rules are irrelevant to the conduct of military operations by the parties to the conflicts in both countries. In this regard, the third paragraph of the UN Convention's preamble declares that a basic purpose of this Convention and its Land Mines Protocol is to give effect to two fundamental customary principles of the laws of war, namely, the rights of the parties to an armed conflict to adopt methods or means of warfare are not unlimited and the use of weapons, projectiles or material calculated to cause superfluous injury or unnecessary suffering is prohibited. Further, another customary principle of the laws of war -- the protection of the civilian population against the effects of hostilities -- is recited in the Convention's second preambulatory paragraph.

76

These principles were expressly recognized in U.N. General Assembly Resolution 2444[16] *Respect for Human Rights in Armed Conflicts* which was adopted by unanimous vote on January 13, 1969. This Resolution's Preamble clearly states that these fundamental humanitarian law principles apply "in all armed conflicts," i.e., both international and internal armed conflicts. The International Committee of the Red Cross has long regarded these principles to be among the basic rules of the laws of war that apply in *all* armed conflicts. And, the U.S. government also has expressly recognized these principles "as declaratory of existing customary international law."[17]

In addition, the inclusion of what is known as the de Martens clause in the U.N. Convention's fifth preambulatory paragraph is not without legal significance. This clause states in pertinent part:

> ... in cases not covered by this Convention and its annexed Protocols or by other international agreement, *the civilian population and the combatants shall, at all times, remain under the protection and authority of the principles of international law derived from established custom, from the principle of humanity and from the dictates of public conscience ....* (Emphasis supplied.)

The principle of humanity, which both complements and inherently limits the doctrine of military necessity, is defined in the U.S. Air Force's *Pamphlet on the Conduct of Armed Conflict and Air Operations* as resulting "... in a specific prohibition against unnecessary suffering and a requirement of proportionality ... [it] also confirms the basic immunity of the civilian population and civilians from being objects of attack during armed conflict ...."[18]  The U.N. Convention's allusion to the principle of humanity reaffirms the customary international law rule, enshrined in G.A. Resolution 2444, which prohibits such attacks against civilians in internal armed conflicts.[19]

These customary principles of the laws of war constitute legal obligation for the warring parties to the internal armed conflicts in El Salvador and Nicaragua.  Furthermore, if these same principles are embodied, reaffirmed or implemented in the provisions of the Land Mines Protocol, then those provisions, independently of the Protocol, could be regarded as part of the customary laws of war and, as such, directly bind the parties to internal armed conflicts.  Accordingly, the following analysis of the Protocol's provisions will particularly focus on this inquiry.

### The Land Mines Protocol

#### Purposes and Dangers of Land Mine Warfare

Unlike other international agreements that limit the use of specific conventional weapons for the protection of both combatants and civilians, the Land Mines Protocol seeks essentially to protect civilians from the dangers of land mine warfare,[20] but does not prohibit the use of these and related devices against military personnel and other military objectives.  There are certain peculiarities to land mines that differentiate their use from that of other conventional weapons.  A U.S. law of war expert notes in this regard:

Unlike ordinary munitions, land mines and booby-traps are not designed to explode when they approach the target. They are, instead, designed to lie dormant until enemy vehicles or personnel approach them. While most munitions are intended primarily to destroy enemy property or personnel, land mines are, in contrast, used primarily to impede enemy access to certain areas of land by requiring mine clearance before those areas are used. Militarily, minefields are similar to ditches, tank traps, and concertina barbed wire in that they are obstacles to enemy movement.[21]

Thus, it is the particular area of land, not the vehicles or persons entering it, that is the object of attack by mines. If the area of land where the mines are placed meets the test of a legitimate military objective, the death or injury suffered by combatants and civilians alike when entering that minefield are collateral or secondary to the primary military purpose for the mines' emplacement.

There are two significant dangers which land mines pose particularly to civilians. One is their possible emplacement in areas populated by civilians; the other concerns those mines that do not self-destruct, but remain active and in place after their military purpose has ceased, thereby presenting a continuing threat to civilians.

The chief purpose of the Land Mines Protocol is precisely to shield civilians from these and other dangerous effects of land mine warfare. The provisions of Articles 2 and 3 of the Protocol implement this purpose (1) by providing definitions of terms necessary for clarifying the obligatory distinction between civil-

79

ians and civilian objects and combatants and other military objectives; (2) by imposing legal restraints, namely a prohibition of indiscriminate use and the rule of proportionality, on land mine attacks directed against military objectives; and (3) by requiring precautionary measures in the use of these weapons in order to avoid or minimize civilian casualties or damage to civilian objects collateral to attacks against military objectives. Other legal restrictions which vary with the type of mine or device, are detailed in Articles 4, 5 and 6 of this instrument.

Before analyzing these articles, however, it should be noted that many of their provisions reaffirm or directly incorporate rules and principles found in comparable articles of Protocol I to the 1949 Geneva Conventions.[22] Thus, authoritative interpretations of these articles can provide relevant standards for interpreting and, possibly, broadening the content of the Land Mines Protocol's articles. Further, to the extent that these provisions of Protocol I affirm or embody customary rules of the laws of war applicable to *all* armed conflicts, these provisions could be considered as customary law. Accordingly, comparable provisions in the Land Mines Protocol could also be regarded as such and, therefore, appropriate for application, where relevant, to the internal armed conflicts in Nicaragua and El Salvador.

## General Prohibitions and Restrictions on Weapons Use

The fundamental rule in the Land Mines Protocol which immunizes civilians from direct attack is stated in Article 3(2), which prohibits in all circumstances the "direct" use, "either in offense, defense or by way of reprisals," of land "mines," "booby-traps," and "other devices" against "the civilian population or individual civilians." The terms "mines," "booby-traps" and "other devices" are defined in Article 2 of the Protocol as follows:

1. 'Mine' means any munition placed under, on or near the ground or other surface area and designed to be detonated or exploded by the presence, proximity or contact of a person or vehicle and 'remotely delivered mine' means any mine so defined delivered by artillery, rocket, mortar or similar means or dropped from an aircraft.

2. 'Booby-trap' means any device or material which is designed, constructed or adapted to kill or injure and which functions unexpectedly when a person disturbs or approaches an apparently harmless object or performs an apparently safe act.

3. 'Other devices' means manually-emplaced munitions and devices designed to kill, injure or damage and which are actuated by remote control or automatically after a lapse of time.

**Civilians and the Civilian Population**

Although the Land Mines Protocol does not define the terms "civilian population" and "individual" civilians, the meaning of these terms is found in Article 50 of Protocol I to the Geneva Conventions. The term "civilian population" is therein defined as comprising "all persons who are civilians" and a "civilian is defined negatively as anyone who is not a member of the armed forces or of an organized armed group of a party to the conflict."

81

These definitions are also relevant for distinguishing civilians from combatants in internal armed conflicts governed by Protocol II to the Geneva Conventions. In this regard, Article 13[23] of Protocol II, like Article 3 of the Land Mines Protocol, merely refers to "individual civilians" and the "civilian population," and this Protocol does not explicitly define combatants as does Article 43 of Protocol I. However, Article 1 of Protocol II contains the basic elements of the concept of armed forces in its allusion to the "armed forces of the High Contracting Party" and to "dissident armed forces or other *organized* armed groups ... under responsible command." The authors of *The Commentary on the 1977 Protocols to the 1949 Geneva Conventions*[24] state that, "inferentially these terms recognize the essential conditions prescribed under Article 43 of Protocol I:  that the armed forces be linked to one of the parties to the conflict; that they be organized, and that they be under responsible command."[25] They conclude significantly that "it thus follows that civilians are all persons who are not members of organizations meeting these qualifications."[26] Accordingly, therefore the civilian population[27] comprises all other persons who do not actively participate in the hostilities -- which means participating in an attack which is intended to cause physical harm to enemy personnel or objects. In addition, the authors of the *Commentary* indicate that the term civilian also includes the following:

> Persons directly linked to the armed forces, including those who accompany the armed forces without being members thereof, such as civilian members of military aircraft crews, supply contractors, members of labor units, or of services

responsible for the welfare of the armed forces, members of the crew of the merchant marine and the crews of civil aircraft employed in the transportation of military personnel, material or supplies.

Civilians employed in the production, distribution and storage of munitions of war, and

Civilians who are taking, or have taken, part in hostilities without combatant status. These persons, however, lose their immunity from attack while they are taking a direct part in hostilities.[28]

Civilians in this latter category, during such time as they assume a combatant's role, should also not be protected by the Land Mines Protocol in internal hostilities.

Article 50 of Protocol I also provides that "the presence within the civilian population of individuals who do not come within the definition of civilians does not deprive the population of its civilian character." The point of this provision, according to the *Commentary*, is that "[t]he presence of a small number of off-duty combatants, or even of some engaged in the transaction of business for the armed forces within a community of civilians would *not subject that community to attack.*[28] (Emphasis supplied.) Such a community, should be similarly immune from direct attack by land mines and related weapons.

### Military Objectives

Another example of definitional coincidence is the meaning ascribed to the term "military objective." Both Protocols define such objectives only as they relate to objects, rather than to personnel, and without designating specific categories of property or persons as military objectives. "Military objective" is defined in Article 2(4) and Article 52(2) of the Land Mines Protocol and Protocol I, respectively, as "any object which by its nature, location, purpose or use makes an effective contribution to military action and whose total or partial destruction, capture or neutralization, in the circumstances ruling at the time, offers a definite[30] military advantage."

Since there is no question that enemy combatants, their weapons, convoys, installations, depots and supplies would be military objectives under Protocol I, these same objects would also qualify as such under the Land Mines Protocol. Moreover, in view of the fact that it is usually an area of land that is the object of a mine attack, such a land area can be a legitimate military objective under both Protocols. The authors of the *Commentary* indicate that objects generally used for civilian purposes, "such as a dwelling, a bus, a fleet of taxi cabs, or a civilian air-field or railroad siding can become a military objective if its location or use meets the criteria set forth in Article 52."[31] Such objects also should be amenable to direct mine attack in accordance with other provisions in the Land Mines Protocol.

### Civilian Objects

The term "civilian objects" is also defined identically in both instruments[32] as "all objects which are not military objectives" as so defined in the same articles. By implication, therefore, all objects should be considered civilian under the Land Mines Protocol, unless they make an effective contribution to the

84

enemy's military action and unless destroying, capturing or neutralizing them, in the circumstances ruling at the time, offers a definite military advantage.

In addition, Article 52(3) of Protocol I creates in doubtful situations, a presumption that objects normally dedicated to civilian use, such as a church, house, or school, are not being used to make an effective contribution to military action. This presumption attaches only to objects which ordinarily have no communication systems, for example, these would not be such objects, and, accordingly, could be legitimate military targets under the criteria of Article 52. This presumption and its application should also operate for similar purposes under the Land Mines Protocol. Further, the definition of civilian objects in Article 52 of Protocol I would also govern the designation of such objects and the extent of their protection under Article 13 of Protocol II.

### Prohibition of Indiscriminate Weapons Use

The rules for the protection of civilians and civilian objects from the effects collateral to the use of land mines against military objectives are stated in Article 3(3) of the Protocol. This article prohibits the "indiscriminate" use of these weapons which is defined as any placement of such weapons:

(a) which is not on, or directed at, a military objective; or

(b) which employs a method or means of delivery which cannot be directed at a specific military objective; or

(c) which may be expected to cause incidental loss of civilian life, injury to civilians, damage to civilian objects, or a combination thereof, which would be excessive in relation to the concrete and direct military advantage anticipated.

This definition is an adoption of the prohibition against indiscriminate attacks as similarly illustrated by examples in Article 51(4) and (5) of Protocol I. Article 3(3), moreover, like Article 51(4) "does not prohibit all [land mine uses] which are of a nature to strike military objectives and civilians or civilian objects without distinction,"[33] but only those specified in subparagraphs (a) (b) and (c). In this connection, the authors of the *Commentary* note that the reference in Article 51(4)(b) to "methods [of attack] which cannot be directed at a specific military objective prohibits 'blind' weapons which cannot, with any reasonable assurance, be directed against a military objective."[34] Significantly, they state that "[l]and mines, laid without customary precautions, and which are unrecorded, unmarked, or which are not designed to destroy themselves within a reasonable time, may also be blind weapons in relation to time."[35]

Subparagraph 3(c) of Article 3 indicates that a target's legitimacy as a military objective does not provide unlimited license to attack it by expressly applying the principle of proportionality for the protection of civilians against the collateral effects of such attacks. Thus, a use of land mines against a military objective which may be expected to cause excessive civilian casualties and damages in relation to the concrete and direct military advantage anticipated would be, by definition, a prohibited indiscriminate use. This express codification of the rule of proportionality implements and clarifies the customary principle

86

of humanity which is applicable to internal armed conflicts and which is alluded to in the Preamble of additional Protocol II.

### Feasible Precautions Requirement

A requirement that all "feasible precautions be taken to protect civilians from the effects of weapons is found in Article 3(4) of the Land Mines Protocol. Such precautions are defined as those "which are practicable or practically possible taking into account all circumstances ruling at the time, including humanitarian and military considerations."

This requirement, which is not expressly clarified by examples, inferentially refers to customary principles of the laws of war which require the attacking party to observe certain precautions when attacking military objectives in order to avoid or minimize collateral civilian casualties. It also refers to provisions in other articles of the Land Mines Protocol which call for actually warning the civilian population of the deployment of land mines on or in an area containing military objective(s). This feasible precautions requirement, thus, complements the obligation of the attacking party to respect the principle of distinction set forth in Article 3(2) of the Land Mines Protocol.

Article 57(2) of Protocol I contains a systematic codification of these customary precautionary rules providing "combatants with uniformly recognized guidance as to their responsibility to civilians and civilian objects in carrying out attacks against military objectives."[36] In this regard, the *Commentary* notes that Article 57(2)(a)[37] "imposes three distinct duties on commanders who decide upon attacks and staff officers who plan an attack: (1) verify that the target of an attack is a lawful military objective, (2) avoid, or in any event, minimize civilian casualties, and (3) ensure that any unavoidable civilian casualties are not excessive in relation to the concrete and direct military advantage anticipated."[38] It adds that in drafting subparagraph 2(a)(i) dealing with verification of legitimate military targets and the rule of proportionality, "the word 'feasible' ... was preferred to 'reasonable' and that it is understood to mean 'that which is practicable or practically possible'".[39] In fact, several delegations expressed understandings "to the effect that as used in Protocol I, 'feasible' means 'that which is practical or practically possible taking into account all the circumstances at the time, including those relevant to the success of military operations.'"[40] This is essentially the same terminology used in the Land Mines Protocol to define "feasible precautions."

The obligations in Article 57[41](2)(a) to avoid collateral civilian casualties and, thus, to refrain from launching attacks that could do so reinforce the principle of proportionality and the protection of the civilian population from the indiscriminate use of land mines in Article 3 of the Land Mines Protocol. In addition to these precautionary measures, Article 57(2)(6) requires that an attack be suspended or cancelled if it becomes evident that the target is not a military objective. This precaution is also appropriate to land mine warfare since its observance is indispensable to compliance with Article 3(a)'s requirement that these weapons only be used on, or directed at, military objectives. Finally, those measures for warning civilians of the presence of land mines are noted in the following discussion of specific restrictions on the use of different kinds of weapons.

## Restrictions on Non-Remotely Delivered Land Mines, Booby-Traps and other Devices

Article 4(2) of the Land Mines Protocol prohibits the use of mines which are "not remotely delivered," namely, hand delivered mines, "booby-traps" and "other devices" in:

> any city, town, village or other area containing a similar concentration of civilians in which combat between ground forces is not taking place or does not appear to be imminent, unless either:
>
> (a) they are placed on or in the close vicinity of a military objective belonging to or under the control of an adverse party, or
>
> (b) measures are taken to protect civilians from their effects, for example, the posting of warning signs, the posting of sentries, the issue of warnings or the provision of fences.

This prohibition does *not* extend, therefore, to any city, town or village where combat between ground forces is taking place or where such combat appears imminent.

Moreover, even if such combat were not occurring or imminent, these mines and other explosive weapons could, nonetheless, be used "on or in the close vicinity of a military objective belonging to or under the control of an adverse party." Carnahan writes that this particular exception "would, for example, permit the destruction of an enemy military objective,

89

located in a city, by a commando force using demolition charges. Alternatively, the raiders could lawfully place mines or booby-traps around the object to prevent its use."[42]

In addition, these weapons can be deployed in peaceable civilian locales if "measures are taken to protect civilians from their effects, for example, the posting of warnings signs, the posting of sentries, the issue of warnings or the provision of fences." Carnahan notes that this language "requires that *some* measures be taken to protect civilians, but does not guarantee the 'effectiveness' of these measures."[43]

Although these exceptions largely obviate the basic prohibition against these weapons' deployment in peaceable civilian concentrations, their permissible use under Article 4 still remains subject to the substantive restraints and prohibitions imposed by Article 3 of the Protocol on their use.

### Restrictions on Remotely Delivered Mines

Article 5[44] of the Protocol establishes a special regime regulating the use of remotely delivered mines[45] which are defined in Article 2(1) as any mine "delivered by artillery, rocket, mortar or similar means or dropped from an aircraft."[46]

Article 5(1) prohibits the use of these mines except "within an area which is itself a military objective or which contains military objectives," and then not unless "their location can be accurately recorded" in accordance with the Protocol, *or* unless each mine has a "self-actuating" or a "remotely-controlled" mechanism which will render the mine harmless or causes its (self) destruction when the mine no longer serves its intended military purpose. Paragraph 2 of Article 5 imposes the additional requirement of effective advance warning of any delivery or dropping of these mines which may "affect the civilian population, unless circumstances do not permit." These restrictions, moreover, are in addition to the general restrictions and prohibitions in Article 3 of the Protocol.[47]

The recording requirement alluded to in Article 5 is stated in Article 7(1)(a) of the Protocol as follows: "The parties to a conflict shall record the location of all pre-planned minefields laid by them." Although the term "pre-planned" is not defined in the Protocol, Carnahan notes:

> Since "pre-planned" means more than "planned," a "pre-planned" minefield is, by its nature, one for which a detailed military plan exists considerably in advance of the proposed date of execution. Naturally, such a detailed military plan could not exist for the vast majority of minefields emplaced during wartime. In the heat of combat many minefields will be created to meet immediate battlefield contingencies with little "planning" or "pre-planning."[48]

The advance notification requirement in Article 5(2) is a *verbatim* incorporation of Article 57(2)(c) of Protocol I. As such, it reinforces the argument that Protocol I's precautionary rules can provide authoritative guidance for interpreting the "feasible precautions" requirements in the Land Mines Protocol.[49] Carnahan suggests that "among the 'circumstances' which might not permit prior warning would be the necessity for tactical surprise or guarding the safety of the aircraft dropping remotely delivered mines."[50]

91

## Particular Restrictions on Booby-Traps

Booby-traps are defined in Article 2(2) of the Land Mines Protocol as "any device or material which is designed, constructed or adapted to kill or injure and which functions unexpectedly when a person disturbs or approaches an apparently harmless object or performs an apparently safe act." In addition to the general restrictions on their use in Articles 3 and 4 of the Protocol, Article 6 places specific prohibitions on the use of certain booby-traps.

For example, Article 6(1)(a) proscribes in all circumstances the use of "any booby-trap in the form of an apparently harmless portable object which is specifically designed and constructed to contain explosive material and to detonate when it is disturbed or approached." This rule would thus forbid the use of mass-produced "pre-fabricated" booby-traps, as well as remotely delivered booby-traps dropped *en masse* from aircraft.

Article 6(1)(b) also prohibits "in all circumstances" the use of booby-traps "in any way attached to or associated with:"

(i)    internationally recognized protective emblems, signs or signals;

(ii)   sick, wounded or dead persons;

(iii)  burial or cremation sites or graves;

(iv)  medical facilities, medical equipment, medical supplies or medical transportation;

(v)  children's toys or other portable objects or products specially designed for the feeding, health, hygiene, clothing or education of children;

(vi)  food or drink;

(vii)  kitchen utensils or appliances except in military establishments, military locations or military supply depots;

(viii)  objects clearly of a religious nature;

(ix)  historic monuments, works of art or places of worship which constitute the cultural or spiritual heritage of peoples;

(x)  animals or their carcasses.

While these prohibitions may appear unrelated, they, in fact, share "a common policy of reinforcing the respect and protection which international law already accords to civilians, cultural property and the sick and wounded."[51]  For example, the care and protection guaranteed to the wounded and sick by the Geneva Conventions, the two 1977 Protocols and common Article 3 would be clearly violated by attaching these devices to such persons.  Under clause (i), it also would be prohibited to use these devices against or on medical and religious personnel, and on medical units and transports which display the Red Cross or Red Crescent emblem.  Moreover, booby-trapping medical transports would be tantamount to using them "to commit hostile acts, outside of their humanitarian function," thereby depriving these objects of their protection under the Second Geneva Convention, and both 1977 Protocols.[52]

The protection of the civilian population from catastrophic effects of warfare is also reinforced by clause (i). Since this provision prohibits the use of these devices in or on internationally recognized signs, "it would forbid the placement of booby-traps on those dams, dikes and nuclear power stations entitled to be marked with "a special sign" under Article 56(7) and Article 15[53] of Protocol I and II, respectively. Under both Protocols, these installations enjoy protection against attacks which might release "dangerous forces" with consequent "severe losses among the civilian population." This protection, however, does not extend to attack by anti-personnel weapons which could not release such forces. Under the circumstances, defenders could use defensive mines and booby-traps against, for example, an infantry attack.

The prohibitions against booby-trapping articles ordinarily used by civilians in clauses (v),[54] (vi), (vii), and (x) also strengthen existing legal restraints on means and methods of warfare which are designed to protect civilians in all armed conflicts. For instance, the forbidden use of these devices on "food or drink," or "animals" implements the policy underlying Article 14 of Protocol II which prohibit attacking or destroying "foodstuffs" and "other objects indispensable to the survival of the civilian population" for the specific purpose of denial for its sustenance value.

El Salvador and Nicaragua are bound by other treaties to give special protection to those cultural and religious objects mentioned in clauses (viii) and (ix). Under Article 16 of Protocol II, the parties to the Salvadoran conflict are prohibited "to commit any acts of hostility directed against historic monuments, works of art of places of worship which constitute the cultural or spiritual heritage of peoples, and to use them in support of the military effort." Article 16 is patterned on Article 53 of Protocol I, except for its omission of any reference to reprisals. Both articles implicitly provide for the loss of these objects' special protection if they are used to support the military effort. The *Commentary* states, however, that this effort must meet the test for military objectives before these protected objects can be attacked.[55]

The 1954 Hague Convention for the Protection of Cultural Property in the Event of Armed Conflict,[56] to which Nicaragua is a party,[57] governs the protections which the parties to the internal conflict there must accord these objects. Article 19 of this Convention, like common Article 3, obligates each party to a conflict not of an international character "to apply" as a minimum, "the provisions of the ... Convention which relate to respect for cultural property."[58] In contrast to Article 16 of Protocol II which covers a limited class of objects which are "part of the cultural and spiritual heritage of mankind," the 1954 Hague Convention requires the warring factions in Nicaragua to give greater protection to a far broader scope of cultural and artistic objects.[59] Further, the Convention prohibits reprisals in internal hostilities, but Protocol II does not. Thus, the booby-trapping of these objects would violate the prohibition against their use for military purposes.

Article 6(2) forbids the use of booby-traps "designed to cause superfluous injury or unnecessary suffering." The unqualified application of this fundamental principle of the law of war to booby-traps would clearly prohibit their use for this purpose in all internal armed conflicts. It should be noted that Article 7(1)(6) requires the parties to a conflict to record the location of "all areas" in which they have made large-scale and pre-planned use of booby-traps.

Based on the preceding analysis of the Protocol's provisions, it is apparent that these provisions in the Protocol that prohibit the direct use of these explosive weapons against the civilian population and individual civilians and that prohibit the indiscriminate use of these weapons againt military objectives for the protection of civilians and civilian objects reaffirm and implement the obligatory rules stated in UNGA Resolution 2444 (XXIII), which is, itself, declaratory of existing customary law applicable to internal armed conflicts. Therefore, as general reaffirmations of these customary rules, these provisions in the Protocol may be regarded as part of the customary laws of war and thereby constitute legal obligations for the parties to the internal hostilities in Nicaragua and El Salvador. Furthermore, the express recognition of the principle of humanity in the UN Weapons Convention's Preamble also requires application of the principle of proportionality in the use of these weapons against military objectives in these internal armed conflicts.

In addition, many provisions of the Land Mines Protocol are patterned on or directly incorporate rules found in comparable articles of Protocol I and Protocol II to the Geneva Conventions. These articles also implement the basic rules of UNGA Resolution 2444 by strengthening and clarifying the principle of civilian immunity and the principle of distinction and by placing legal restrictions on attacks. As general restatements of these

96

basic rules, these articles should also be regarded as customary law. And, as explained in the *Commentary* and in previous Americas Watch reports on Nicaragua[60] and El Salvador,[61] the customary rules in UNGA Resolution 2444 are either inferentially or directly embodied in provisions of Protocol II to the Geneva Conventions which, together with common Article 3, constitute part of the law governing the hostilities in El Salvador. Accordingly, those provisions of the Land Mines Protocol which incorporate or reinforce these provisions of Protocol I and II, should similarly be regarded as customary law and applied, where appropriate, to the internal armed conflicts in Nicaragua and El Salvador.

Finally, to insure their compliance with those provisions of the Land Mines Protocol constituting customary law, the parties to the conflicts in Nicaragua and El Salvador should respect and implement the Protocol's other normative rules in the expectation that these rules will become part of the customary laws of war which will bind all states.

**Application of Relevant Provisions of the Land Mines Protocol to the Armed Conflicts in El Salvador and Nicaragua**

Based on the preceding examinations of relevant legal rules, we can make the following statements:

I. **Civilians** - The following persons in Nicaragua and El Salvador should be considered civilians and, thus, not subject to direct attack by land mines, booby-traps and related devices:

1. The peaceful population not directly participating in hostilities;

2. (a) Persons providing only indirect support to the Salvadoran or Nicaraguan army by *inter alia*, working in defense plants; distributing or storing military supplies in rear areas, supplying labor and food, or serving as messengers or disseminating propaganda. These persons may *not* be subject to direct individualized attack since they pose no immediate threat to the adversary. However, they assume the risk of incidental death or injury arising from the use of these weapons against legitimate military targets.

   (b) Persons providing such indirect support to the *contras* in Nicaragua or to rebel groups in El Salvador are clearly subject to prosecution under domestic laws of their respective countries for giving aid and comfort to the enemy.

3. Persons (not members of the parties' armed forces) who do not actually take a direct part in the hostilities by trying to kill, injure or capture enemy combatants or to damage material. These civilians, however, lose their immunity from attack for such time as they assume a combatant's role. Included in this category would be armed civilian members of the Nicaraguan self-defense groups who guard rural cooperatives, farms and plants against *contra* attack.

II. **Civilian Objects** - For purposes of both armed conflicts, the following should be considered civilian objects immune from direct attack by these weapons in Nicaragua and El Salvador:

1. Structures and locales, such as a house, churches, dwelling, school, farm, village and cooperatives, which in fact are exciusively dedicated to civilian purposes and, in the circumstances prevailing at the time, do not make an effective contribution to military action.

2. In El Salvador, those historic monuments, works of art or places of worship constituting the cultural or spiritual heritage of peoples, provided they are not used to support the enemy's military effort.

3. In Nicaragua, those buildings, monuments and other objects defined as "cultural property" by the 1954 Hague Convention for the Protection of Cultural Property, provided their special protection is not waived for imperative military necessity.

III. **Military Objectives** - While not an exhaustive list, the following persons, groups and objects may be regarded as legitimate military objectives subject to direct attack by weapons specified in the Land Mines Protocol:

1. In Nicaragua
   (a) Members of the Popular Sandinista Army and Militias
   (b) Members of ARDE, FDN, KISAN, and MISURASATA

2. In El Salvador
  (a) Members of the Salvadoran combined armed forces and civil defense forces
  (b) Members of the FMLN

3. In both countries
  (a) Weapons, other war material, military works, military and naval establishments, supplies, vehicles, camp sites, fortifications, and fuel depots or stores which are or could be utilized by either party to the conflict.
  (b) Objects which, while not directly connected with combat operations, effectively contribute to military operations in the circumstances ruling at the time, such as transportation and communication systems and facilities, airfields and ports and otherwise non-military industries of importance to the ability of a party to the conflict to conduct military operations, such as raw or processed coffee destined for export in Nicaragua.

IV. **Prohibited Uses of Weapons** - Although not an all encompassing list, the following uses of land mines, booby-traps and related devices should be prohibited in the conduct of hostilities in both countries:

1. Their direct use against individual or groups of unarmed civilians where no legitimate military objective, such as enemy combatants or war material, is present. Such uses of these weapons are indiscriminate.

100

2. The direct use against civilian objects, i.e., towns, villages, dwellings or buildings dedicated to civilian purposes where no military objective is present. Such weapons' use is also indiscriminate.

3. The use of any remotely delivered mines which are not effectively marked and have *no* self-actuating or remotely controlled mechanism to cause its destruction or neutralization once its military purpose has been served. Such mines are "blind weapons" and their use is indiscriminate as to time.

4. The use of hand delivered mines, such as Claymore varieties, and booby-traps in or near a civilian locale containing military objectives which are deployed *without* any precautions, markings or other warnings, or which do *not* self-destruct or are *not* removed once their military purpose has been served. Such uses are similarly indiscriminate.

5. The use of mass-produced pre-fabricated booby-traps, as well as remotely delivered booby-traps dropped *en masse* from aircraft.

6. The use of booby-traps in the guise of "letter-bombs." Such use is indiscriminate.

7. The use of booby-traps designed to cause superfluous injury or unnecessary suffering, such as hidden pits

containing poisoned objects.

8. The direct use against medical and religious personnel, medical units and transports, particularly when they are recognized as such by the display of the distinctive emblem of the Red Cross or Red Crescent.

9. The use of booby-traps either attached to or associated with:

   (a) sick, wounded or dead persons, including combatants who are captured, surrendered or *hors de combat*;

   (b) burial or cremation sites or graves;

   (c) medical facilities, equipment, supplies or transports;

   (d) articles ordinarily used by or for the care, hygiene, health or education of children under fifteen years of age;

   (e) food or drink; animals or their carcasses;

   (f) to defend those dams, dikes and nuclear power stations entitled to be marked with internationally recognized signs;

   (g) in El Salvador, those historic monuments, works of art or places of worship constituting the cultural or spiritual heritage of peoples;

(h) in Nicaragua, those buildings, monuments and other objects defined as "cultural property" by the 1954 Hague Convention for the Protection of Cultural Property.

## V. Classification of Civilian Casualties

1. The deaths and injuries of civilians as a result of the prohibited or indiscriminate use of these weapons may be properly classified as homicides or felonious assaults attributable to the responsible party to the conflict.

2. The deaths and injuries of civilians when they directly participate in hostilities should be classified as combat related, since they forfeit their immunity from direct attack.

3. The deaths and injuries of civilians who, because they are near or located within a legitimate military objective, are killed or injured as a result of direct attack against such objectives should be classified as combat related. Since such persons assume the risk of death or injury arising from such attacks, their deaths are collateral or incidental to the primary purpose of these weapons' use.

It is important to note that the limitations noted herein on the use of these *particular* conventional weapons are in addition to and apply simultaneously with those other humanitarian law restrictions, noted in prior Americas Watch reports, governing the use of *all* conventional weapons in the Salvadoran and Nicaraguan conflicts.

# ENDNOTES

1. Starting before the war, in the mid-1970s, peasants began to leave their homes, prompted by threats and assassinations by local civil defense and paramilitary groups. Others left for political reasons or were forced out by local landlords; yet others fled to government-controlled zones when the FMLN moved in and threatened and killed those who had taken actions against FMLN supporters. More than 500,000 Salvadorans have been displaced within the country over the past seven years and an even larger number have fled the country entirely.

2. Using the press as the sole source for human rights information, without further investigation, makes a mockery of human rights reporting, as we have pointed out on various occasions. COPREFA, the Armed Forces' press office in the headquarters of the Joint Chiefs of Staff, should not be expected to serve as an objective source of information on casualties, even its own. This is not unique to the Salvadoran Armed Forces, of course; it is in the nature of military forces in any armed conflict to make information subordinate to propaganda. The Armed Forces casualty figures were graciously made available to us by the Joint Chiefs of Staff in a document labelled "secret." The document presented detailed lists of civilian injuries and deaths by FMLN mines from January 1, 1984 to August 2, 1986, but its figures were lower than Tutela Legal's (counting all victims), the U.S. Embassy's (COPREFA's), and the government Human Rights Commission's. We cannot explain the discrepancy.

3. Here, we refer only to deaths in cases where Tutela Legal was able to carry out investigations. As we have noted in previous reports, we regard these figures compiled by Tutela Legal as particularly solid. Tutela Legal also compiles figures indicating a much larger number of predominantly civilian deaths occurring in the course of military operations in circumstances where Tutela Legal was unable to carry out on-site investigations. Because such investigations were not carried out, these must be considered much softer figures.

4. Tutela Legal (and by extension Americas Watch, which reports Tutela Legal's figures) have come under criticism for not gathering statistics on civilians injured by mines. We are aware of no criticism for our failure to gather statistics on civilian injuries from operations in which government forces were exclusively or principally involved, such as bombings, strafings, shelling or groundsweeps.

5. Unfortunately, the government Human Rights Commission does not accompany its statistics with names, dates and places, as does Tutela Legal, and as the government Commission itself does with civilian mining victims. The government Commission would improve its credibility and the usefulness of its work by including such detailed information, not only on victims of FMLN abuses, but also of government abuses. It would also provide a valuable service by indicating what action is taken by the government, be it through the Armed Forces, security forces, or judicial system, to punish those responsible for these on-going offenses.

6. On an August 1986 spot visit to the main hospital in San Salvador, we found just two mining victims, although the nurses told us there had been others who had been discharged. In San Miguel we found seven mining victims in one day, as well as a woman who had been wounded by a soldier-thrown grenade; the soldier threw the grenade, which killed the woman's son, because the woman's daughter had rejected his advances. In the hospital in San Vicente the nurses told us there had been mining victims earlier in the year, but none had come in for several months.

   We suspect that military personnel benefit from longer hospital stays than civilians because, unlike the civilians, they usually benefit from prosthetic devices and rehabilitation.

7. We did not obtain a comparable figure of soldiers injured by mines in 1985, but from the numbers available from the Military Hospital, it is obvious that military mining injuries have risen sharply. Throughout 1985, 1278 soldiers entered the hospital with injuries from explosives, arms fire, and projectiles. Of these, 301 represented injuries from gun accidents, always a major source of military casualties; the remaining 977 wounded included injuries by hostile fire as well as by mines. This figure, which covered the entire year, has already been surpassed by the 1006 wounded by mines alone for the first eight months of 1986.

8. This young man was recuperating from surgery in the Military Hospital in San Salvador and willingly spoke to us from his hospital bed. He had been severely injured when his unit was ambushed while he was in the act of deactivating a guerrilla mine. We found him a credible witness. He received his explosives training in a 45-day course given in August 1985 by Salvadoran experts. He was assigned to a specialized unit that placed and removed Armed Forces mines and deactivated FMLN mines.

106

9. Despite several written requests, Americas Watch did not obtain permission to visit a Nicaraguan military hospital or to speak to a military mining expert or a military doctor. We were denied entry to the main military hospital at Apanas even after a civilian official said it had been arranged.

10. The texts of these instruments are reprinted in U.N.G.A. Doc. A/Conf. 95/15 and Corr 1-5; and in 19 Int'l Legal Materials 1534 (1980). The Convention and its three Protocols entered into force on 2 December 1983 (hereinafter "Land Mines Protocol"). The Convention is an "umbrella" treatly to which are attached three optional protocol agreements, each of which contains specific limitations on the use of particular conventional weapons. In addition to the Land Mines Protocol, the other two protocols concern Non-detectable Fragments (Protocol I) and Prohibitions or Restrictions on the Use of Incendiary Weapons (Protocol III). Under this structure, the Convention's provisions apply to all three protocols. At the time a state ratifies or accepts the Convention, it must indicate its consent to become bound by at least two of these protocols. Thereafter, the state can become a party to the other protocol. (Article 4(3)(4) of the UN Convention).

11. Article 2 common to the Geneva Convention for the Amelioration of the Condition of the Wounded and Sick in Armed Forces in the Field, Aug. 12, 1949, 6 U.S.T. 3114, T.I.A.S. No. 3362, 75 U.N.T.S. 31; Geneva Convention for the Amelioration of the Condition of the Wounded, Sick and Shipwrecked Members of the Armed Forces at Sea, Aug. 12, 1949, 6 U.S.T. 3217, T.I.A.S. No. 3363, 75 U.N.T.S. 85; Geneva Convention Relative to the Treatment of Prisoners of War, Aug. 12, 1949, 6 U.S.T. 3316, T.I.A.S. No. 3364, 75 U.N.T.S. 135; Geneva Convention Relative to the Protection of Civilian Persons in Time of War, Aug. 12, 1949, 6 U.S.T. 3516, T.I.A.S. No. 3365, 75 U.N.T.S. 287.

12. Article 1 paragraph 4 refers to ... armed conflicts in which peoples are fighting against colonial domination and alien occupation and against racist regimes in the exercise of their right of self determination, as enshrined in the [U.N.] charter Declaration of Principles of International Law Concerning Friendly Relations and Cooperation Among States in accordance with the charter ....

Protocol additional to the Geneva Conventions of 1949, and relating to the Protection of Victims of International Armed Conflicts (Protocol I), [hereinafter Protocol I]; reprinted in U.N.G.A. Doc. A/32/144, Anns. I and II, 15 Aug. 1977 and in 16 Int'l Legal Materials 1391 (1977).

13. Nicaragua signed the Convention on May 20, 1981.

14. The International Committee of the Red Cross (ICRC) has stated that the provisions of Article 3 possess now the character of jus cogens, i.e., a peremptory norm of international law, and thus are binding on all authorities claiming to exist in international law. See speech of Jacques Moreillon, Director for General Affairs and Directorate Member, ICRC, entitled "International Humanitarian Law and Terrorism" at the Inter-American Seminar on State Security, Human Rights and Humanitarian Law, San Jose Costa Rica, September 1982.

Article 3 reads as follows:

> In the case of armed conflict not of an international character occurring in the territory of one of the High Contracting Parties, each party to the conflict shall be bound to apply, as a minimum, the following provisions:

> (1) Persons taking no active part in the hostilities, including members of the armed forces who have laid down their arms and those placed hors de combat by sickness, wounds, detention, or any other cause, shall in all circumstances be treated humanely, without any adverse distinction founded in race, color, religion or faith, sex, birth or wealth, or any other similar criteria.

> To this end, the following acts are and shall remain prohibited at any time and in any place whatsoever with respect to the above-mentioned persons:

> (a) violence to life and person, in particular murder of all kinds, mutilation, cruel treatment and torture;

> (b) taking of hostages;

> (c) outrages upon personal dignity, in particular humiliating and degrading treatment;

> (d) the passing of sentences and the carrying out of executions without previous judgment pronounced by a regularly constituted court, affording all the judicial guarantees which are recognized as

108

indispensable by civilized peoples.

(2) The wounded and sick shall be collected and cared for.

An impartial humanitarian body, such as the International Red Cross, may offer its services to the Parties to the conflict.

The Parties to the conflict shall further endeavor to bring into force, by means of special agreements, all or part of the other provisions of the present Convention.

The application of the preceding provisions shall not affect the legal status of the Parties to the conflict.

15. Protocol additional to the Geneva Conventions of 1949, and Relating to the Protection of Victims of Non-International Armed Conflicts (Protocol II) [hereinafter Protocol II]; reprinted in U.N.G.A. Doc. a/32/144, Anns. I and II, 15 Aug. 1977 and in 16 Int'l Legal Materials 1442 (1977). Since Nicaragua is not a party to Protocol II, it does not directly govern the conflict there; however, it provides relevant interpretive standards for the protection of the civilian population in the conduct of hostilities.

Article 1, para 1 of Protocol II limits that instrument's application to non-international armed conflicts "... which take place in the territory of a High Contracting Party between its armed forces and dissident armed forces or other organized armed groups which, under responsible command, exercise such control over a part of its territory as to enable them to carry out sustained and concerted military operations and to implement this Protocol." Thus, the objective conditions which must be satisfied to trigger Protocol II's application contemplate a situation of classic civil war, essentially comparable to a state of belligerency under customary international law.

The International Committees of the Red Cross has expressly recognized the applicability of Protocol II to the Salvadoran conflict in its 1983 Annual Report. See ICRC 1983 Annual Report at 29.

16. This resolution affirms, inter alia:

   ... the following principles for observance by all governments and other authorities responsible for action in armed conflicts:

(a) That the right of the parties to a conflict to adopt means of injuring the enemy is not unlimited;

(b) That it is prohibited to launch attacks against the civilian populations as such;

(c) That distinction must be made at all times between persons taking part in the hostilities and members of the civilian population to the effect that the latter be spared as much as possible.

17. See letter of September 22, 1968, from the General Counsel, U.S. DOD to Senator Edward Kennedy regarding War-related Problems in Indo-China in Rovine, Contemporary Practice of the United States Relating to International Law, 67 AJIL 118, 122-25 (1973). The principles of civilian immunity from direct attack are expressly stated in US Army Field Manual 27-10, para. 25 and in U.S. Air Force Pamphlet 110-131, para. 5-3. See also U.N. General Assembly Res. 2675 (XXV), 1970.

18. Air Force Pamphlet AFP 110-31, International Law -- The Conduct of Armed Conflict Air Operations 1-6 (1976). Similar definitions are contained in FM27-10, at 5 and in U.S. Navy, NWIP 10-2, Law of Naval Warfare 5 (1959).

19. Various provisions in treaties to which El Salvador and Nicaragua are parties also afford the civilian population similar protection. For example, common Article 3's prohibition of "violence to life and person against persons taking no active part in hostilities" (emphasis added) is broad enough to include attacks against civilians in territory controlled by an adverse party. And, in the case of the Salvadoran conflict, individual civilians and the civilian population are expressly immunized from direct attack by Article 13 of Protol II.

20. Article 1 of the Land Mines Protocol limits its material scope of application to "The use on land of the mines, booby-traps and other devices defined herein, including mines laid to interdict beaches, waterway crossings or river crossings, but does not apply to the use of anti-ship mines at sea or in inland waterways." The Protocol, therefore, does not affect existing international laws governing mine warfare at sea.

110

21. Carnahan, The Law of Mine Warfare: Protocol II to the United Nations Convention on Certain Conventional Weapons, 105 Military L. Rev., 73, 75 (1984). (Hereinafter "Carnahan").

22. Carnahan notes "[t]hat delegates to the weapons conference uniformly turned to the 1949 Geneva Conventions and the 1977 Protocols for definitions, terminology and basic principles of law. The 1949 Geneva Conventions and the 1977 First Protocol are, therefore, to be considered in para materia with the Land Mines Protocol." Carnahan supra note 12 at ft. nt. 6 at 74.

23. Article 13 states:

    1. The civilian population and individual civilian shall enjoy general protection against the dangers arising from military operations. To give effect to this protection, the following rules shall be observed in all circumstances.

    2. The civilian population as such, as well as individual civilians, shall not be the object of attack. Acts or threats of violence the primary purpose of which is to spread terror among the civilian population are prohibited.

    3. Civilians shall enjoy the protection afforded by this Part, unless and for such time as they take a direct part in hostilities.

    It is also important to note that the detailed rules in Protocol I apply only to international armed conflicts and are not, for the most part, replicated in additional Protocol II. However, these rules are relevant for interpreting the substantive content of similar, less detailed provisions in Protocol II.

24. M. Bothe, K. Partsch & W. Solf, New Rules for Victims of Armed Conflicts -- Commentary on the Two 1977 Protocols Additional to the Geneva Conventions of 1949 at 627 (1982) (hereinafter "Commentary"). This volume is presently the authoritative legal treatise which interprets and explains the provisions of the two Protocols.

25. Id. at 672.

26. Id.

27. Article 8 of the Land Mines Protocol accords similar protections to members of UN Missions and peacekeeping forces -- persons who are not included within the scope of this report.

28. "Commentary" supra note 15 at 293-294.

29. Id at 296.

30. Contextually, "definite" means a concrete and perceptible military advantage, rather than a hypothetical or speculative one. See Commentary supra note 15 at 296.

31. Id. at 306-307.

32. Protocol I, Art. 52(1); Land Mines Protocol, Art. 2(5). Although there is no express provision in Protocol II affording general protection for civilian objects, the authors of the Commentary state that "... the protection against direct attack of paragraph 2 [Art.13], also precludes attacks against civilian objects used as dwellings or otherwise occupied by civilians not then supporting the military effort." Commentary supra note 15 at 677.

33. Commentary supra note 15 at 305.

34. Id.

35. Id.

36. Id. at 360.

37. Article 57(a)(2) states:

With respect to attacks, the following precautions shall be taken:

(a) those who plan or decide upon an attack shall:

(i) do everything feasible to verify that the objectives to be attacked are neither civilians nor civilian objects and are not subject to special protection, but are military objectives within the meaning of paragraph 2 of Article 52 and that it is not prohibited by the provisions of this Protocol to attack them;

(ii) take all feasible precautions in the choice of means and methods of attack with a view to avoiding, and in any event to minimizing, incidental loss of civilian life, injury to civilians and damage to civilian objects;

(iii) refrain from deciding to launch any attack which may be expected to cause incidental loss of civilian life, injury to civilians, damage to civilian objects, or a combination thereof, which would be excessive in relation to the concrete and direct military advantage anticipated;

(b) an attack shall be cancelled or suspended if it becomes apparent that the objective is not a military one or is subject to special protection or that the attack may be expected to cause incidental loss of civilian life, injury to civilians, damage to civilian objects, or a combination thereof, which would be excessive in relation to the concrete and direct military advantage anticipated;

(c) effective advance warning shall be given of attacks which may affect the civilian population, unless circumstances do not permit.

38. Commentary supra note 15 at 362.

39. Id.

40. Id.

41. Id. at 363. Further, under Article 57(a)(i), the obligation to do everything "feasible" to verify that a target is a military objective involves "a continuing obligation to assign a high priority to the collection, collation, evaluation and dissemination of timely target information."

42. Carnahan supra note 12 at 81.

43. Id. He also indicates that some government delegations to the conferences which elaborated the Protocol "believed that guerrilla fighters would meet the requirements of this rule [Article 4(2)(b)] by orally informing the civilian

113

population of the location of mines and booby-traps, without disclosing the location of these munitions to enemy troops." Id. at 81-82.

44. Article 5 states:

1. The use of remotely delivered mines is prohibited unless such mines are only used within an area which is itself a military objective or which contains military objectives, and unless:

   (a) their location can be accurately recorded in accordance with Article 7(1)(a); or

   (b) an effective neutralizing mechanism is used on each such mine, that is to say, a self-actuating mechanism which is designed to render a mine harmless or cause it to destroy itself when it is anticipated that the mine will no longer serve the military purpose for which it was placed in position, or a remotely-controlled mechanism which is designed to render harmless or destroy a mine when the mine no longer serves the military purpose for which it was placed in position.

2. Effective advance warning shall be given of any delivery or dropping of remotely delivered mines which may affect the civilian population, unless circumstances do not permit.

45. Delayed action bombs may well come within the definition remotely delivered mines. Carnahan supra note 12 at ft. not. 29 at 75.

46. 'Aircraft' includes helicopters, drones, remotely-piloted vehicles, and balloons. Id. at ft. nt. 29 at 79.

47. Carnahan notes that since these mines can be rapidly laid behind enemy lines, there were fears that their indiscriminate emplacement could threaten the civilian population. There was, therefore, "... an express understanding that all the general restrictions on mine warfare in Article 3 also applied to remotely-delivered mines." Id. at 80.

48. Id. at 84. He also notes that the recording requirement applies only to the location of pre-planned minefields, not to the location of individual mines therein, or to the composition or configuration of the mines within the field.

114

49. Id. Consequently, the Working Group on Land Mines drafted the following non-binding technical annex of recording guidelines which, if complied with, will meet the recording obligations under Article 7:

> Whenever an obligation for the recording of the location of minefields, mines and booby-traps arises under the Protocol, the following guidelines shall be taken into account.
>
> 1. With regard to pre-planned minefields and large-scale and pre-planned use of booby-traps:
>
>     (a) maps, diagrams or other records should be made in such a way as to indicate the extent of the minefield or booby-trapped area; and
>
>     (b) the location of the minefield or booby-trapped area should be specified by relation to the co-ordinates of a single reference point and by the estimated dimensions of the area containing mines and booby-traps in relation to that single reference point.
>
> 2. With regard to other minefields, mines and booby-traps laid or placed in position:
>
>     In so far as possible, the relevant information specified in paragraph 1 above should be recorded so as to enable the areas containing minefields, mines and booby-traps to be identified. Id. at 83-84.

50. Id. at 80. Carnahan's view is supported by similar examples in the Commentary on Article 57(2)(c).

51. Carnahan supra note 12 at 91.

52. See Second Convention, Art. 39; Protocol I, Art. 23; Protocol II, Art. 11. Such conduct would violate implicitly common Article 3's guarantee that "the wounded and sick shall be cared for." Carnahan observes regarding clause (i) that "[t]he reference to objects using protective 'signals' would apply ... to medical aircraft using radio or light signals as authorized by Article 18 of the 1977 First Protocol." Id.

115

53. Unlike Article 56(7) of Protocol I, Article 15 is silent on the use of the international sign for identification purposes. However, according to the Commentary, the absence of an express provision "... does no harm. As there is no restriction on the use of the sign in peacetime, there can be no objection to its use in time of internal armed conflict for the purpose of facilitating recognition of protected status." Commentary supra note 15 at 685.

54. Although not defined in the Land Mines Protocol, the term "children" is referred to in Articles 14 and 38 of the Fourth Geneva Convention and Article 77 of Protocol I as "children under fifteen." Inferentially, clause (v) also applies to individuals under fifteen.

55. Commentary supra note 15 at 333. This statement referred to Article 53 and inferentially applies to Article 16 of Protocol II.

56. May 14, 1954, 249 U.N.T.S. 240.

57. Nicaragua ratified the Convention on November 25, 1956.

58 These obligations are stated in Article 4 as follows:

> Art. 4. 1. The High Contracting Parties undertake to respect cultural property situated within their own territory by refraining from any use of the property and its immediate surroundings or of the appliances in use for its protection for purposes which are likely to expose it to destruction or damage in the event of armed conflict; and by refraining from any act of hostility directed against such property.
>
> 2. The obligations mentioned in paragraph 1 of the present Article may be waived only in cases where military necessity imperatively requires such a waiver.
>
> 3. The High Contracting Parties further undertake to prohibit, prevent and, if necessary, put a stop to any form of theft, pillage or misappropriation of, and any acts of vandalism directed against, cultural property.
>
> 4. They shall refrain from any act directed by way of reprisals against cultural property.

59. Under Article 1 of the Convention, the term "cultural property" includes

irrespective of origin or ownership:

(a) movable or immovable property of great importance to the cultural heritage of every people, such as monuments of architecture, art or history, whether religious or secular; archaeological sites; groups of buildings which, as a whole, are of historical or artistic interest; works of art; manuscripts, books and other objects of artistic, historical or archaeological interest; as well as scientific collections and important collections of books or archives or of reproductions of the property defined above;

(b) buildings whose main and effective purpose is to preserve or exhibit the movable cultural property defined in sub-paragraph (a) such as museums, large libraries and depositories of archives, and refuges intended to shelter, in the event of armed conflict, the movable cultural property defined in subparagraph (a);

(c) centres containing a large amount of cultural property as defined in sub-paragraphs (a) and (b), to be known as "centres containing monuments."

60. See AW, Violations of the Laws of War by Both Sides in Nicaragua 1981-85 (March 1985) at pp. 11-34 ("1985 Nicaragua Report").

61. See AW, Protection of the Weak and Unarmed: The Dispute Over Counting Human Rights Violations in El Salvador (Feb. 1984) at pp. 30-45. ("1984 El Salvador Report").

117